Life in Communist
Russia

Titles in The Way People Live series include:

THE WAY PEOPLE LIVE

Life in Communist Russia

Russia

by
Thomas Streissguth

Lucent Books, P.O. Box 289011, San Diego, CA 92198-9011

Library of Congress Cataloging-in-Publication Data

Streissguth, Thomas, 1958–
    Life in communist Russia / by Thomas Streissguth.
        p. cm. — (The way people live)
Includes bibliographical references and index.
    ISBN 1-56006-378-5 (alk. paper)
    1. Soviet Union—Social life and customs—Juvenile literature. [1. Soviet
Union—Social life and customs.] I. Title. II. Series.
    DK266.4 .S77 2001
    947—dc21

                                                                00-010405

Contents

Discovering the Humanity in Us All

Books in The Way People Live series focus on groups of people in a wide variety of circumstances, settings, and time periods. Some books focus on different cultural groups, others, on people in a particular historical time period, while others cover people involved in a specific event. Each book emphasizes the daily routines, personal and historical struggles, and achievements of people from all walks of life.

To really understand any culture, it is necessary to strip the mind of the common notions we hold about groups of people. These stereotypes are the archenemies of learning. It does not even matter whether the stereotypes are positive or negative; they are confining and tight. Removing them is a challenge that's not easily met, as anyone who has ever tried it will admit. Ideas that do not fit into the templates we create are unwelcome visitors—ones we would prefer remain quietly in a corner or forgotten room.

The cowboy of the Old West is a good example of such confining roles. The cowboy was courageous, yet soft-spoken. His time (it is always a he, in our template) was spent alternatively saving a rancher's daughter from certain death on a runaway stagecoach, or shooting it out with rustlers. At times, of course, he was likely to get a little crazy in town after a trail drive, but for the most part, he was the epitome of inner strength. It is disconcerting to find out that the cowboy is human, even a bit childish. Can it really be true that cowboys would line up to help the cook on the trail drive to grind coffee, just hoping he would give them a little stick of peppermint candy that came with the coffee shipment? The idea of tough cowboys vying with one another to help "Coosie" (as they called their cooks) for a bit of candy seems silly and out of place.

So is the vision of Eskimos playing video games and watching MTV, living in prefab housing in the Arctic. It just does not fit with what "Eskimo" means. We are far more comfortable with snow igloos and whale blubber, harpoons and kayaks.

Although the cultures dealt with in Lucent's The Way People Live series are often historically and socially well known, the emphasis is on the personal aspects of life. Groups of people, while unquestionably affected by their politics and their governmental structures, are more than those institutions. How do people in a particular time and place educate their children? What do they eat? And how do they build their houses? What kinds of work do they do? What kinds of games do they enjoy? The answers to these questions bring these cultures to life. People's lives are revealed in the particulars and only by knowing the particulars can we understand these cultures' will to survive and their moments of weakness and greatness.

This is not to say that understanding politics does not help to understand a culture. There is no question that the Warsaw ghetto, for example, was a culture that was brought about by the politics and social ideas of Adolf

Hitler and the Third Reich. But the Jews who were crowded together in the ghetto cannot be understood by the Reich's politics. Their life was a day-to-day battle for existence, and the creativity and methods they used to prolong their lives is a vital story of human perseverance that would be denied by focusing only on the institutions of Hitler's Germany. Knowing that children as young as five or six outwitted Nazi guards on a daily basis, that Jewish policemen helped the Germans control the ghetto, that children attended secret schools in the ghetto and even earned diplomas—these are the things that reveal the fabric of life, that can inspire, intrigue, and amaze.

Books in The Way People Live series allow both the casual reader and the student to see humans as victims, heroes, and onlookers. And although humans act in ways that can fill us with feelings of sorrow and revulsion, it is important to remember that "hero," "predator," and "victim" are dangerous terms. Heaping undue pity or praise on people reduces them to objects and strips them of their humanity.

Seeing the Jews of Warsaw only as victims is to deny their humanity. Seeing them only as they appear in surviving photos, staring at the camera with infinite sadness, is limiting, both to them and to those who want to understand them. To an object of pity, the only appropriate response becomes "Those poor creatures!" and that reduces both the quality of their struggle and the depth of their despair. No one is served by such two-dimensional views of people and their cultures.

With this in mind, The Way People Live series strives to flesh out the traditional, two-dimensional views of people in various cultures and historical circumstances. Using a wide variety of primary quotations—the words not only of the politicians and government leaders, but of the real people whose lives are being examined—each book in the series attempts to show an honest and complete picture of a culture removed from our own by time or space.

By examining cultures in this way, the reader will notice not only the glaring differences from his or her own culture, but also will be struck by the similarities. For indeed, people share common needs—warmth, good company, stability, and affirmation from others. Ultimately, seeing how people really live, or have lived, can only enrich our understanding of ourselves.

The People and the State

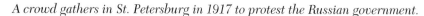

In March 1917, as the people of Russia demonstrated against the hunger and privations brought by World War I, the tsar of the Russian Empire gave up his throne. A provisional government took power in St. Petersburg, the imperial capital. Seven months later, the Bolshevik wing of the Russian Socialist Party led the overthrow of the provisional government. Under Vladimir Ilich Ulyanov, known to history by his revolutionary name of Lenin, the Bolsheviks transformed Russia into a socialist state, modeled on the ideas of the nineteenth-century writers Karl Marx and Friedrich Engels.

Like Marx and Engels, Lenin saw history as a logical, scientific process. The aim of the Bolshevik government would be to bring this process to its natural conclusion: a socialist state of perfect equality and justice. At this final point in the process, communism would be attained; government itself would no longer be needed, and the state would gradually "wither away," as Engels predicted in his book *The Origin of Family, Private Property, and the State*:

When it [the state] ultimately becomes really representative of society as a whole,

A crowd gathers in St. Petersburg in 1917 to protest the Russian government.

it makes itself superfluous. Government over persons is replaced by administration of things and the direction of procuring production. The state is not abolished; it withers away.[1]

Before withering, the state would have to guide the people on their path to communism. For example, the leaders of the state, working in committees, would control manufacturing, farming, and the entire national economy by careful planning. They would decide where people would live, what schools they would go to, what they would do for a living, and what information they would have. They would decide on the appropriate books, movies, music, and art. There would be no private property to be used and exploited by individuals for their selfish personal gain. Instead, all land and property would belong to the state. The government would own all factories and farms on behalf of the people, and operate them in the most productive manner possible.

According to Marxist-Leninist theory, the workers were the masters of this new system. As the new bosses, the workers controlled production and made decisions through their soviets (councils) of elected representatives. The Bolsheviks set up a soviet for nearly every organization of people with any purpose whatsoever, including schools, factories, and farms. Every city, and every neighborhood, had its decision-making council, as promised by the revolutionary slogan, "All power to the Soviets!"

After surviving a civil war, the Bolshevik revolution spread to every corner of the far-flung Russian Empire. Lenin moved the capital from St. Petersburg to Moscow, the largest city of Russia. The Bolsheviks organized Ukraine, Belarus, and other parts of the empire into separate republics and, on December 30, 1922, founded the Union of Soviet Socialist Republics, or the Soviet Union.

Life Turned Upside Down

As the largest republic within the Soviet Union, Russia held most of the country's population, fertile land, and resources. Lenin and most of the other leaders of the Bolshevik revolution were Russians, and the Communist experiment began earlier and progressed faster in Russia than in the other republics. The government seized factories and shops from former bosses, claimed homes from their former owners, and requisitioned livestock and grain from Russian farmers. All forms of communication and information came under state control. With no property and no future prospects under Bolshevik rule, millions of people left the country.

The Bolsheviks knew that many Russians still opposed their revolution. To enforce the new system, the Soviet government set up a secret police organization known as the Cheka. The name *Cheka* came from a Russian acronym meaning "Extraordinary Committee to Combat Counterrevolution and Sabotage." The Chekists set up a vast network of informers to find out what ordinary people were doing and whether these people remained loyal to the revolution. On every block and in every neighborhood, citizens of Communist Russia carefully watched each other for signs of disloyalty to the revolution or criticism of the new regime. As a result, ordinary Russians grew fearful of expressing their opinions and mistrustful of their friends and neighbors.

With the assistance of the Cheka, the Bolsheviks turned Russia into the world's first

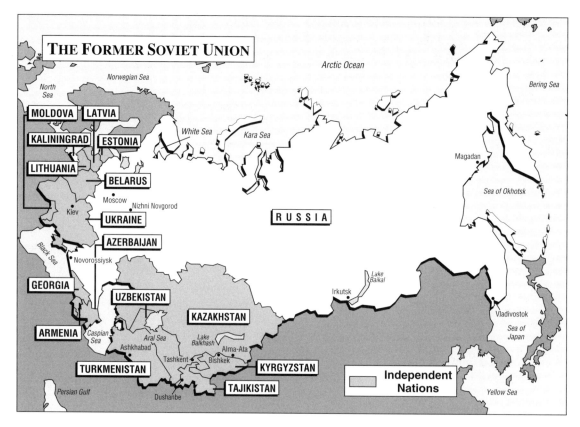

THE FORMER SOVIET UNION

Independent Nations

socialist state. Later, the Cheka would undergo a transformation of its own, becoming first the NKVD, then the KGB. Operating from a large headquarters building in the heart of Moscow, the KGB remained one of the largest and most important divisions of the Soviet government.

A Historic Experiment

The people of Russia participated in a historic experiment, a test of the theories of Marx, Engels, and Lenin. They made up a vanguard, and their success or failure in this experiment would be seen as the success or failure of socialism and the Communist utopia. Convinced that capitalism would fail because of its exploitation of the workers,

many people in Russia strongly believed in communism and were willing to make any sacrifice, and commit any act of injustice or violence, to see it through.

In a conversation with a friend, Georgy Solomon, Lenin himself expressed this intent to destroy traditional Russia completely in order to achieve the Communist utopia:

> Yes, we are going to tear the whole thing down! We shall destroy and smash everything, ha-ha-ha, with the result that everything will be smashed to smithereens and fly off in all directions, and nothing will remain standing!
>
> Yes, we are going to destroy everything, and on the ruins we will build our temple! It is a temple for the happiness of all! [2]

Most importantly, Lenin and his followers believed that all Russians shared a common purpose—one much greater and more noble than the desire for money, material things, and security. In Communist Russia, such striving appeared disloyal and unpatriotic. Individual ambitions had to be left behind in order to attain the goals of the state, which claimed to represent the collectivity of the people. All individuals had to work, study, and live for the collective interest, and the state blamed any failures of the socialist state, any stumbling on the road to communism, on those who lacked this commitment.

In Communist Russia, no facet of ordinary life—work, school, recreation, religion, athletics, or entertainment—escaped the application of "Marxist-Leninist" dogma. As a result, communism trained the Russian people to see all of their actions in a political light, a fact of life that carried certain dangers. When Joseph Stalin ruled the Soviet Union during the 1930s and 1940s, for example, activities that are taken for granted in free societies could be punished by imprisonment, exile to forced labor camps, or execution.

Russia's socialist state did raise living standards for millions of people, and also improved health, education, and literacy. Through a crash program of industrialization, Russian workers also transformed their country from a largely rural and poverty-stricken land into a mighty industrial power, a "superpower," in just a few decades. But inefficiency,

According to Lenin (left) and Marx (right), workers in the Communist system would control their own productivity for the good of the collective state.

Socialism and Communism

The Bolshevik revolution of 1917 brought radical changes in the way Russians saw their own society and the societies of other countries. Those who supported the revolution believed that Russia had just taken a giant step forward in the natural evolution of human societies. They now lived under socialism—a system of collective ownership of all land and property. The term *socialist* had its origins in the movement for better and fairer working conditions for European industrial workers in the early eighteenth century.

Socialism, however, was but a single step on a long road to communism. It was a difficult step, requiring the people to give up their material wants, as well as their liberty, in the quest for the ideal they were striving for, the last stage of social evolution according to the model of Marx and Lenin. Once communism was reached, the nation would prosper and all Russians would be able to satisfy their needs and wants. Even government would be unnecessary.

People outside of Russia often confused the terms *socialism* and *communism*, but to Russians the meanings were clear and distinct. They lived in a socialist nation and carried out their functions as members of a socialist economic system. They lived under a Communist Party government dedicated to promoting socialist revolutions all over the world, wherever conditions were ripe. Once real communism—that is, a just and self-sufficient society of equals—was achieved, the Communist Party government was expected to declare itself no longer needed and disband.

economic stagnation, and corruption also marked the Marxist-Leninist state. In fact, corruption and lawlessness moved to every level of society, for it was only by breaking the law that the individual citizen could follow his or her natural instincts and try to get ahead. And it was only by joining the Communist Party that one could secure a position of authority and obtain the most highly desired goods and privileges—particularly the privilege of traveling outside the country.

As a result, Communist Russia did not achieve a state of equality and justice for all of its citizens. Instead, it created a nation where the vast majority of people felt excluded from, and threatened by, their own government. It also resulted in an economic disaster in which citizens of a vast and resource-rich land struggled to provide their families with the bare necessities of life and comfort. The socialist ideas of Marx and Lenin turned out to be better suited as a study for writers and philosophers than a system to be imposed on millions of human beings, with all of their varying abilities, ambitions, and interests.

1 Life in the City

Lenin and other Soviet leaders understood that urbanization and industrialization were the key to the success of their endeavor. Marx himself had seen socialism as a system most suited to modern, Western European countries such as England, France, or Germany. In these countries, history had progressed the furthest on its logical, predictable path toward communism. Industrial workers living in large cities would carry out the revolution, and from the urban working class would come the leaders of the new socialist society.

But Russia remained a largely agricultural nation into the 1930s. Then, after World War II (1939–1945), rapid urbanization took place. The state built hundreds of new cities from the ground up and millions of Russian farmers left the countryside to take up new jobs as factory workers. Russia did not reach a majority urban population until the 1960s. By the mid-1980s, two-thirds of all Russians were living in cities.

City Life and Living Places

To encourage urbanization, Russia's Communist rulers built hundreds of new cities, intended to serve as models for the Communist utopia of the future. The typical new city had

As a result of the emphasis on urbanization, large apartment structures were built near factories in the larger cities

Joining the Party

One of the original goals of socialism was to create a classless society. There would no longer be any bosses lording over ordinary workers; instead, the workers would take charge, collectively, for the common good. They would run the state through their soviets, which would take charge of production, education, housing, and cultural life. Decisions made by elected representatives of the workers, according to Marx and Lenin, would prove the wisest and most beneficial to society at large.

Nevertheless, class divisions remained after Russia was transformed into a socialist state. The main divide was a very simple one: membership or nonmembership in the Communist Party. In order to join the party, two individuals had to vouch for the candidate's loyalty. A local party committee then decided whether to accept or reject the application.

When accepted, the new member was granted a party card, which bore a number. The first party members held cards with the lowest numbers, and thus had more prestige as longtime Communists. The very first number—000001—belonged to Vladimir Ilich Ulyanov. Party card number 000002 belonged to Leonid Brezhnev, who served as first secretary of the Communist Party, and leader of the Soviet Union, during the 1960s until his death in 1982.

its focus in a single heavy industry, such as auto manufacturing or steelmaking, which employed most of the city's inhabitants. The new cities also followed a basic plan, and a visitor traveling from one town to the next might feel a sense of never having left home. As described by Michael Dobbs in his book *Down with Big Brother*, these model cities were

> uniform in their soul-destroying drabness, gridlike layouts, and pompous style of municipal architecture. Lenin Avenue always led up to Lenin Square, dominated by a huge statue of Lenin, right arm thrust up in classic taxicab-hailing pose. The biggest building in each square was always the headquarters of the local Communist party, and the party secretary [chief] always had his offices on the second floor. Faded propaganda banners—with slogans like "Glory to the Communist Party" and "We Promise to Fulfill the Goals of the Five-Year Plan"—adorned the potholed streets. [3]

In Communist Russia, the government legally owned all homes and apartment buildings. To enforce the ban on private property, the state evicted millions of families and seized their living quarters after the revolution. Those found loyal to the state, or those enjoying personal connections to the authorities, had the best chance at being granted a spacious and private place to live. Others placed their names on the state's waiting lists. It could take ten years, or longer, to be permitted to move to a new home or apartment, but it was possible to jump ahead on the lists by offering bribes, exchanging favors, or pulling the right strings.

Ironically, in Communist Russia the homes and apartments built before the revolution became the most desirable places to live. Many of these older buildings displayed fine architectural details, such as high doorways and windows, marble steps and floor tiles, and even chandeliers. Their inhabitants sometimes had the services of doormen and chauffeurs, as well as caretakers who kept the plumbing, electricity, and elevators in good working order. The best buildings were reserved for authority figures: factory managers, government officials, and prestigious scientists and doctors. The rent was the same as that for a communal apartment, but these apartments were impossible for ordinary workers to obtain.

Apartments built during the Communist regime displayed little individuality. Generally, the Communist government considered any display of individuality to be "decadent," and architects worked accordingly. Millions of people lived in tall, monotonous concrete buildings, raised in vast housing parks that encircled the country's urban centers. In these collectivist buildings, most dwelling spaces were small, cramped, poorly lit, and badly insulated. In common areas outside the apartment, hallways, sidewalks, and light fixtures deteriorated, and untended parks and lawns sprouted weeds, trash, and dust.

The majority of Russians lived in communal apartments, in which more than one family shared the limited space. Communal apartments became a way of life for most Russian city dwellers. Each family within the communal apartment claimed a single room, or a portion of a room, and arranged itself as comfortably as possible.

The Collective Way

The communal apartment threw complete strangers into intimate, daily contact with each other. Within these small dormitories, the most valued possession was a few square meters of private space for reading, talking, or listening to the radio. Communal apartment dwellers had to negotiate the use of heat and electricity, the responsibility for cleaning, and the use of halls and bathrooms. In the kitchen, which served as the apartment's common area, each

The communal apartment (pictured) forced strangers to dwell in close proximity to each other.

family owned its own pots, its own dishes, and its own line for hanging laundry. Each family also claimed its own small table and cupboard.

The communal apartment represented a miniature of the Communist ideal: the collective way of life. According to this philosophy, the members of society should not live on their own, concerned only with their own wants and needs and isolated from each other. Instead, in the ideal socialist state, no citizen required more than a private place to sleep and change clothes. Collectivism was supposed to bring about mutual concern and assistance and bring about a better life for all. But in most cases, the communal apartment brought contention, not cooperation. One Russian woman named Lusya complained,

> Of all the horrible perversions invented by the Soviet system, the communal apartment is the most horrible perversion of them all. It destroys the boundary between the outer world and the inner, the public and private. You open the door of your room and you're in Red Square.[4]

Conflicts over the use of space, cleanliness, noise, and eating arrangements became everyday occurrences. Personal habits became public, forcing apartment dwellers to either accept or fight against those traits that disturbed them: holding parties, inviting late-night guests, listening to the radio, even snoring. Mutual suspicion grew as families fought for some comfort and a little privacy. In his book *Soviet Civilization: A Cultural History* Andrei Sinyavsky describes a typical situation under such conditions in the 1950s:

> In the kitchen, every pot on the stove was under lock and key. To stir the soup or to taste it, one had to unlock the pot and then relock it, for fear a neighbor might filch a piece of meat—less from hunger than from spite—or slip something into it: extra salt, dirt from the floor, or just some spit. . . . This gives one a sense of the tension of life in a communal apartment.[5]

In Communist Russia, every aspect of daily life, and not just living quarters, was to be shared in a collective manner. There were collective recreational facilities, reading rooms, dining halls, and child-rearing centers. But, as Sinyavsky writes,

> Even a person raised in the spirit of collectivism wants a corner of his own, his own saucepan, lunch at home with his family and, finally, his solitude. It is impossible, as we know, to live without society, but to be always surrounded by others is a heavy burden.[5]

Goods and Services

Although Russians might complain about privacy, they had fewer reasons to worry about the cost of living. Under socialism, the state fixed the low prices of basic goods as well as utility rates and rent, all of which remained affordable for ordinary workers. As a result, however, apartment dwellers who could claim little private property of their own lived very wastefully. Lights were kept on, and in many apartments radios and televisions operated almost continuously. In the winter, ovens were used to heat kitchens. Food was readily thrown away or allowed to spoil.

When apartment dwellers needed to arrange repairs to appliances or plumbing, another difficulty arose. Like all other laborers, repair workers were employed by the state. Because their skills were in high demand, and their salaries were fixed no matter how much or how little they accomplished, they had little incentive to show up on time or to perform good work. Often, those needing repairs had to offer bribes of money or food in order to see the work begun and completed. Frequent bribes of vodka, the strong liquor preferred by Russians, brought about drunkenness, tardiness, and shoddy work.

Once outside the apartment, and in search of goods to buy, the people of Communist Russia participated in another important aspect of their new system: the line. In the cities, lines developed everywhere, along nearly every busy street and thoroughfare. Lines formed in front of bakeries and grocery stores, furniture shops, repair shops, and sidewalk kiosks that sold tickets and information. Citizens had to wait in long lines for admission to public baths, restaurants, museums, theaters, and cinemas. From time to time, the average Russian had to devote an entire day to waiting in lines.

The lines were brought about by the system of distributing goods. Public authorities controlled distribution without regard to the demand for goods in a particular city or neighborhood. Constant shortages of bread, meat, toilet paper, light bulbs, shoes, hats, coats, and hundreds of other items resulted. Any item not easily obtained was known as a "deficit" item (food items that Russia had to import, such as citrus fruits, were always deficit items). Deliveries of such goods occurred randomly, without notice to the public. Whenever such a delivery was made, a line formed in front of the shop that sold it. Those joining the line, hoping to reach the sales counter before the store again ran out, knew that they might have to wait a long time for another opportunity to buy the deficit goods.

Russian shoppers carried cash and a shopping bag wherever they went, just in case a promising line was spotted. They might stand in line for hours or keep up a system of substitution, in which one friend or family member replaced another to wait in the line for a certain amount of time. Many people joined lines without knowing what item was being waited for; rumors spread up and down

Because of constant shortages of consumer goods, shoppers in Communist Russia regularly waited in long lines for them.

the lines. Places in line were jealously guarded, and line-jumping sparked ill will, arguments, and fights.

For large consumer goods, waiting in line to purchase something could actually take months. Harrison Salisbury, an American journalist who lived for many years in the Soviet Union, described the procedure in which the eager buyer

gets in line on a given day and when he gets to the top of the line, which may take many hours, he registers his name in the queue. This gives him the right to a given place, but he must turn up at regular intervals and stand in line for several hours, or perhaps all day, in order to preserve his place. He may have to stand one day a month or one day a week—whatever is the rule of the given organized queue. Then, as he gradually works his way up to the top of the line the matter becomes more urgent. Now he will go every day and stand all day in line, just in case something unexpected should happen. An unusual supply of television sets might arrive and he might not be there to pick up his order, in which case he would lose it as well as the months of time and trouble.[7]

Buying basic necessities such as toilet paper or meat became a sort of treasure hunt, in which gossip, rumor, and secrecy played key roles. The most mundane features of daily life became the object of great effort and drama. The drama did not end once the hopeful shoppers reached the inside of the store where the sales clerks who controlled the final distribution of goods to the public often provided very poor service. It was usually necessary to bribe a clerk with gifts, money, or services in return for the chance to obtain under-the-counter goods that were supposed to be available to the public.

One way Russians responded to this way of life was by making jokes about it. The following is a well-known example:

Two Muscovites [people of Moscow] are in a gallery, and they come across a painting of Adam and Eve. One of them says to the other, "Look at that. Adam and Eve. They've got to be Russian." "Why?" asks the other. "They've got nothing to wear; there's nothing to eat but an apple between them. And they think they're in Paradise."[8]

Doing the Business of *Blat*

The wide-ranging system of mutual aid, bribery, and favors—also known as *blat*—was no laughing matter. Every individual in Communist Russia depended on *blat* to get by or to get ahead. Parents offered gifts to teachers in return for giving special attention to their children in school. Patients offered food or favors to clinic doctors in exchange for closer attention to their illnesses or injuries. Store clerks held aside certain hard-to-find goods for customers who could do them a valuable favor in return.

A large part of Russia's economic life was carried out in secret, between friends and acquaintances, on an enormous black market. The black market operated outside the commands of state planners and official committees. Many workers and factory managers illegally diverted their goods outside the state's distribution channels to sell them for a better profit "under the table." Professional black marketers, or *fartsovshschiki*, dealt in foreign goods banned in Russia, such as cigarettes, recorded music, books, and clothing. In this underground trade, dealers accepted foreign currency alongside and sometimes in

Legal Muscovites

Moscow was both the capital and the largest city of the USSR. Ordinary citizens considered living in Moscow a privilege and a great stroke of luck. But those who lived anywhere else in the country couldn't just pick up and move to Moscow. To live there, they had to have a special blue stamp known as a *propiska*, which was placed in an internal passport that all Soviet citizens had to carry. (After a famine swept across the Soviet Union in the early 1930s, millions of people moved to the cities to avoid starving to death. The government created passports in order to control this great flood of domestic immigrants.)

The *propiska* stamp was a coveted item. The police issued them, and they didn't allow peasants, convicted criminals, or those without jobs or apartments to have them. Dissidents—those considered opponents of the regime—also did not have permission to live in Moscow. Anyone caught staying in the city for more than three days without permission could be arrested and sent back where he or she came from, or into exile in Siberia.

---

place of Russian rubles. They obtained many valuable goods directly from tourists, and black-market dealings were especially important in Moscow, Leningrad, and other cities that the state permitted foreigners to visit.

Writer J. N. Westwood describes Sukharevka, a huge black market in Moscow, during the earliest days of the Bolshevik regime:

Here the former propertied classes traded the remains of their possessions for scarce foodstuffs. In time these supplies of fine china, furniture, jewellry, clocks, pianos, ball dresses, silver and paintings were exhausted, and their owners denuded. But new sellers appeared with new commodities: tools, equipment, and materials purloined from government factories and army depots by workers and soldiers. Some private barter was quite legitimate. Since workers were paid largely in kind [i.e., with goods instead of money] there was nothing wrong, say, in a non-smoker selling his tobacco allocation on the Sukharevka.[9]

Nearly everyone in Communist Russia, at one time or another, did business in the underground economy. In many cases, there was no other way to obtain the goods or services that one sought. But engaging in the black market, especially as a professional trader, carried certain risks. Those found guilty of stealing or diverting state property could be punished with long prison terms. Those found guilty of more serious economic crimes, such as embezzlement or forgery, could be shot.

Every day, ordinary citizens who knew about these risks had to walk the fine line between permitted and illegal activity. They put careful calculation into daily activities such as buying, selling, trading, and bartering. The question of their loyalty to the state surrounded their decisions. Actions as ordinary as getting around—whether by taxi, bus, train, or private automobile—also might involve one's attitude toward socialism and the state's "command economy." The fruits of success in these endeavors were a comfortable home, a good education, a well-paid job, and permission to travel.

Getting Around

Travel within Communist Russia was strictly regulated. The state put military bases, official government facilities, and the homes of important officials off limits to ordinary citizens and tourists. For most, travel outside the country was even more difficult. In order to leave Russia, citizens had to obtain official permission and travel in a tour group; no individual travel was allowed. Any disciplinary problems or criminal record, any disagreements with the Communist Party or the government, any black marks on the record of a student or worker, would bring a denial of permission to travel.

Once abroad, Russians ran into another difficult problem: Foreign banks would not exchange their rubles for the local currency (Communist Russia did not allow rubles to be traded on international currency markets; as a result, foreign banks would not buy rubles). To purchase items to bring home, Russians had to use whatever foreign currency they managed to collect, either through the black market or from previous trips abroad. Often, they had to rely on barter—a simple exchange of goods with no money involved.

At home, the majority of Russians traveled either on foot or by public transportation, which included taxis, buses, and streetcars. A subway ran in Moscow, the country's capital and largest city. The state intended the elegant, clean, and safe Moscow subway as an example of its success and prosperity, and Communist officials often compared their subway to such systems in Western Europe and the United States as an example of the superiority of socialism.

At the same time, however, the most basic private automobiles proved too expensive for many Russian families. Russia's largest car, the heavy black Volga sedan, was usually reserved by the state for people in authority. Volgas also made up a large part of the nation's fleet of taxicabs. But the Volga cost the equivalent of seven or eight years' salary for an ordinary worker. Most Russians had to save up several years' earnings just to buy a Zaporozhets, the cheapest car on the market.

Travel within Communist Russia, and especially abroad, was strictly regulated.

A taxi driver stands beside his Volga.

Buying a car meant waiting—sometimes for years. New cars had to be ordered in advance from the factory, and the prospective buyer was placed on a waiting list. Because cars were rare items, older models held their value (an example of supply and demand operating in a state that claimed to have banished the ordinary market economy). Owners could often sell their used cars at the same price they would have commanded when new. Many of those who could not afford cars used a motorcycle or bicycle for private transportation. Two-wheeled vehicles proved especially useful in rural areas where public transportation did not exist.

In Russian cities, many drivers moonlighted as cabbies. Official taxis worked on a meter, but unofficial (and illegal) taxi drivers negotiated prices with passengers. Many professional chauffeurs made a good living after hours as private cab drivers. But black-market drivers had to evade the uniformed agents of the GAI (State Automobile Inspection), the Russian traffic police who patrolled the streets and manned the checkpoints leading out of large cities.

Soviet Secrecy

One serious problem facing Russian drivers and travelers was the lack of good maps. In Communist Russia, the authorities jealously guarded information of all kinds—especially information that might allow state enemies to find their way around the country. Maps sold in Moscow were particularly bad, as Scott Shane recounts in his book *Dismantling Utopia*:

> The maps were useless not because Soviet mapmakers were incompetent. Oil geologists had access to excellent maps, which they were permitted to examine only in certain guarded rooms, no note-taking allowed. Ordinary people's maps were useless because they were designed to be useless. Stalin's NKVD [the state security police] had decreed in the late 1930s that no accurate maps should be given to the public for fear that they would fall into the hands of potential military adversaries.[10]

The tight controls on information reached down into the most mundane occurrences of everyday life. The average citizen did not know why trains or planes were delayed or when stores would be restocked with goods. The state also controlled all newspapers, which printed only news and information the government wanted the public to have. The government did allow coverage of crime, bribery, official incompetence, and so forth, whenever it had a good reason to (for example, during an official campaign against black-market dealings). The problems of the capitalist West, such as poverty and crime, also took up significant space and time in the Soviet media. Secrecy shrouded official decisions and policy, however, as the state deemed such information unnecessary to its citizens.

Even telephone books were a rarity in Moscow. Instead of consulting printed sources, the public had to buy phone numbers, addresses, directions, information about museum hours and cinema showings, and so on from public kiosks, which typically charged a small fee for each piece of information. This system was a legacy of the early Bolshevik leaders, who believed that the strict control of information could only help to bring about the Communist utopia as quickly as possible.

Women in Communist Russia

The vision of the Bolshevik leaders ranged as far as the most intimate details of home and family life. Anatoly Lunacharsky, a "commissar" (director) of education in the 1920s, put it like this:

Our problem now is to do away with the household and to free women from the care of children. It would be idiotic to sep-

arate children from their parents by force. But when, in our communal houses, we have well-organized quarters for children, connected by a heated gallery with the adults' quarters, to suit the requirements of the climate, there is no doubt the parents will, of their own free will, send their children to these quarters, where they will be supervised by trained pedagogical and medical personnel. There is no doubt that the terms "my parents", "our children" will gradually fall out of usage, being replaced by such conceptions as "old people", "adults", "children", and "infants".[11]

The Bolshevik visionaries did not foresee all the effects the Communist experiment would have on Russian women and their families. After the revolution, women enjoyed opportunities that had long been denied them by law and tradition. They could enter universities and travel just as freely as men. They could join the military, and they met no legal barriers to entering professions once exclusively male. Women in Communist Russia worked as doctors, scientists, and engineers.

But communism did not change one very important aspect of life for Russian women: the traditional responsibilities of maintaining a home. Most Russian husbands and fathers did not share the day-to-day responsibilities of cooking, cleaning, and shopping. In addition to providing food and clothing, Russian mothers took care of infants, brought up young children, and supervised teenagers, chores made even more difficult while sharing a communal apartment. In many cases, grandparents helped with child rearing, especially when both parents worked during the day. But for most Russian women, these responsibilities added up to an exhausting daily burden that didn't cease until they reached the treasured nightly allotment of sleep.

Sex Under Communism

As writer Leonid Vladimirov recounts in *The Russians*, the communal apartment inhabited by the average Russian city dweller made certain private matters even more difficult than they were in other societies.

"A major unsettling element in the pursuit of sex and love in the Soviet Union is the lack of privacy. Under the prevailing conditions of overcrowded housing, people are crammed together, with more than one family to a single apartment. It is not hard to see how this kind of ant-heap living can produce discords in even the most lyrical attachment. A young man can not usually hope to spend a few quiet hours at home with his girl friend, even on one of those rare evenings when his parents are out. The vigilant neighbors, with whom the apartment is shared, would be sure to discuss, next day in the kitchen, every sound, verbal and otherwise, that they had detected from the room in which the young man spent his time with the girl. It would not matter how harmlessly the two had spent their hours together. It could be made to seem quite lurid. . . .

Young people will seek seclusion in other people's apartments, lent to them by friends for an hour or two, or in unlit stairways, or in the murky corners of courtyards and attics. The furtive and hasty love experienced in such places is unlikely to abet the higher ideals of romance."

Providing a wardrobe posed difficulties as well. Most Russians owned only a few suits of clothes and could not be picky about fashion. When new lines of shirts, trousers, or dresses arrived in the shops, buyers lucky enough to be on hand snapped them up immediately, since the next shipment might not arrive for months. Friends and family members who had permission to travel abroad were given extensive shopping lists for articles available only in the outside world. The typical Russian housewife also had to be a skilled seamstress. The most treasured articles of clothing—blue jeans either imported or made in Russia—were kept for several years and continually patched.

Such conditions made life difficult for many married couples. About one-third of all marriages in Communist Russia ended in divorce (a rate that remained lower than in many Western countries, including the United States). During the 1920s, the situation was almost chaotic, as J. N. Westwood explains:

At one time it almost seemed that the Bolsheviks were attempting to end the family as a social unit, but in fact only a handful inside the Party envisaged this. However, free love was accepted, and instant divorce and instant marriage were made easy. (Divorce was immediately granted at the request of one of the partners.) Easy divorce and the critical housing situation often resulted in ludicrous and tragic situations. Depending on which of the marriage partners was the legal tenant of the home, a husband or wife could without warning lose both spouse and house. A wife might learn of her divorce only when her husband brought his new wife home. Sometimes the legal tenant would allow the ex-wife or ex-husband to remain. Because in the towns the home consisted usually of a single room, there were cases when a husband and wife slept in the same room with two or three of their previous partners.[12]

Traditional responsibilities of cooking, cleaning, and shopping did not change for women in Communist Russia.

Throughout the duration of Communist Russia, divorce remained legal and easy to obtain. But if a divorce involved children or a dispute over property, the estranged couple had to appear before a judge for arbitration. (Contrary to Lunacharsky's vision, the concept of "our children" did not disappear under the Communist system.) Divorce judges commonly granted custody of children to ex-wives and ordered ex-husbands to make child-support payments.

Doctoring in Communist Russia

One of the most common occupations for the professional Russian woman was working as a physician. For health care, Russians visited neighborhood polyclinics, which provided free or low-cost care and prescriptions to the general public. Most of the doctors staffing these polyclinics were female general practitioners, who occupied the lowest rung of the medical profession. Medical specialists, most of whom were male, enjoyed a much higher status in Russian society. To even obtain an appointment to see a specialist, such as a cardiologist or an eye doctor, the ordinary Russian had to use all of his or her influence and connections.

For common maladies such as colds or the flu, Russian doctors prescribed aspirin and plasters, medicated dressings that were applied to the chest and back. For serious cases, they would also prescribe drugs, but prescription medicines were in short supply and sometimes impossible to buy. A patient who needed an operation was placed on a waiting list for the next opening, which might not occur for another year.

The people of Russia believed in homeopathic medicine and home remedies. They used certain natural preparations, plants, berries, and the like, for different illnesses and injuries. These remedies were passed down from one generation to the next. Old wives' tales also survived the Bolshevik revolution. For example, Russians strongly suspected cold air of carrying disease. They bundled in several layers of heavy wool clothing when outside, wore fur hats on their heads during much of the year, and kept their homes and apartments tightly shut against the winter winds.

Eating and Drinking

Russians had always been adept at preparing food for the long winters. Tomatoes and other vegetables and mushrooms were pickled and kept in glass jars. Apples and other fruits could be preserved as jams or dried. Dried sausages could be kept a long time with minimal refrigeration.

Russians drank tea, milk, and *kvass*, a thick and strong drink fermented from stale bread. The most common alcohol present on Russian tables was vodka, a clear spirit distilled from fermented grain or potatoes. Small glasses of vodka accompanied all sorts of private and public dinners, and the ability to consume large amounts was a source of pride to many Russians. A typical celebration included a series of toasts, accompanied by speeches, after which speakers and listeners tossed off their glasses of vodka, only to have them filled again.

The consumption of vodka posed serious health and social problems for Communist Russia. State-manufactured vodka was plentiful and cheap, and the result was widespread alcoholism throughout the country, in rural as well as urban areas. Alcohol contributed to many of the nation's road accidents and much of its petty crime. Drunken workers were responsible for shoddy goods, poor construction, mishandled repairs, and low production. A good percentage of worker absenteeism was due

State-manufactured vodka was cheap, but the consequences of overconsumption contributed to low productivity and high worker absenteeism.

to drunkenness and hangovers, and chronic, alcohol-related illnesses represented the nation's leading causes of death.

To curb alcohol abuse, the state passed strict laws from time to time. To be caught drinking at all while driving, for example, meant the immediate suspension of one's driver's license. But the leaders of Communist Russia never managed to solve the problem, no matter how many directives and laws were passed. Because their lives were so tightly regulated, and their opportunities limited, many Russians drank out of sheer frustration and boredom. Indeed, throughout the Soviet era, intense dissatisfaction was a common problem among citizens in all walks of life, whether they lived in a busy city or in a quiet, changeless rural village.

Life in the Country

The Bolshevik revolution progressed more slowly in the countryside than it did in the cities. With their livelihoods dependent on small plots, Russian farmers and villagers strongly resisted the collective ownership of their land. Once the new system was firmly established, the people who remained in the country suffered the most from the inefficiencies of the Communist system. Every day, millions of Russian villagers traveled by train and bus to large cities such as Moscow and Leningrad to shop for items that were unavailable in their home towns. Many people from the country even took up temporary residence in the cities, where they lived in train stations, parked cars, and back streets. They spent a few days shopping in the city, then left when their money ran out.

Russia's heart and soul still lay in the countryside, a place where the people observed traditional customs, prepared traditional meals, and followed the Eastern Orthodox religion. To city dwellers experiencing the harsh monotony of the modern Soviet city, the peasants represented the sturdy virtues of old Russia that endured alongside a revolutionary economic and political system.

Getting Away From the City

Russian urbanites took every opportunity they could to travel away from the city and participate in this simpler and quieter traditional life. Because foreign travel was so difficult, they usually spent their vacations and holidays in the country, where many families owned small country homes known as dachas. Surrounded by a little land, often built near a river or lake, the dacha served as a simple and rustic retreat from the noise and bustle of the city.

At the country dacha, vacationers avoided doing much exercise or physical work. Journalist Harrison Salisbury describes typical dacha activities:

> lying in a hammock and reading novels; long talks around a bubbling samovar; quiet walks through the village in the evening twilight; excursions into the pine and birch forests, looking for mushrooms; occasional visits to the village pond for bathing and sun-bathing but not really swimming (very few Russians swim well. They prefer to wade in shallow water or sit and watch others splashing along the shore).[13]

Nearly all Communist officials and leaders also had the use of official government dachas, which ranged in size from small, one-room cottages to elaborate country palaces with several bedrooms, indoor plumbing, and electricity. The largest and most prestigious dachas also had stables and saunas, with several surrounding acres used for small gardens. As Michael Dobbs relates,

> In the elaborate reward-and-punishment system . . . there was no greater prize than

Russians spend their vacations at their dachas in the country.

a country house.... For the Soviet elite—government ministers to nuclear scientists to prima ballerinas to army generals—a dacha was not only a place of rest but a form of escape from the oppressive atmosphere of the capital, with its noxious pollution and paranoid sense of being under constant surveillance.[14]

While staying at their dachas, vacationers also enjoyed rural sports such as hunting and fishing, hiking, and cross-country skiing. A favorite vacation or holiday pastime of all Russians, whether they were city or country dwellers, was gathering mushrooms. This provided the occasion for full-day outings in the vast forests, where large groups of family and friends would pick their way around fallen tree trunks and grassy meadows. Many families had a secret spot for mushroom collecting known only to them. After gathering their fungi in large baskets, they would care-

fully discard poisonous species and keep those that were edible. Russian cooks used wild mushrooms in many of their home-cooked meals.

The Farmer and the Communist System

Spending vacation time in the countryside was a world away from living and working there. In many ways, the problems and conflicts brought by the new state were magnified in rural areas, where peasants had made up 80 percent of Russia's total population before the Communist revolution. Whereas many Russian city workers had fought for and supported the revolution, farmers strongly opposed the Bolshevik regime from the outset. They clung to the Orthodox religion of their parents and ancestors even as Communist officials closed their churches and arrested their priests. They remained suspicious of the Marxist-Leninist utopia of perfect social equality, since most Russian peasants had been serfs—little better than slaves—until the abolition of serfdom just fifty years before the revolution.

Most of all, the Russian farmer objected to the collective ownership of land. Small as many were, the private acreages held by Russian farming families represented their only true wealth, their livelihood, and their defense against starvation and destitution. During a nationwide campaign undertaken during the 1930s, however, the Soviet gov-ernment succeeded in collectivizing Russian agriculture. Collectivization was achieved only by fomenting class warfare; Communist officials were sent to villages to pit landless peasants against those who owned some property, machinery, and livestock. The state withheld food and seized grain from regions that resisted collectivization, a tactic that brought starvation to millions. After this in-duced famine, the government sent loyal peasants to repopulate thousands of empty villages. The collectivization of Russian farmers was one of the most violent episodes in modern Russian history.

Leaving Home

Although millions of hungry and war-weary Russians had supported the Bolsheviks, for most rural landowners, the revolution meant the loss of land as well as home. Con-fiscations began in the 1920s and continued for several years, as dedicated Communists forcibly evicted millions of families consid-ered counterrevolutionaries. One family of the village of Sergiyevskoye, the Osorgins, was abruptly thrown off their estate in 1918, just as the civil war erupted between Red and White armies. Author Serge Schme-mann, in his book *Echoes of a Native Land*, quotes Maria Osorgin describing that terri-ble day.

"We were ousted . . . within three days. We were not even allowed to take anything ex-cept clothes, and where was there time to pack everything in our huge house? We left everything as it was. We arose from break-fast, leaving behind even the bowl with fruits, we went into the living room, where open music still lay on the piano, while in the other rooms, in the billiards room, in the study, the commissars were already acting like masters, lowering the curtains for some reason and putting locks on the doors. We rushed to go out on the stoop, so this would not happen in our presence, but they kept delaying the horses, and there was a terrible moment when we all, dressed, with all our things, sat there on the stoop. I especially remember Papa's face, and we all kept silent, and endlessly and stupidly waited for the delayed cart. At the gates of the yard and the garden there was a mass of peas-ants, who wept and crossed themselves from a distance, but they were forbidden to come in to say goodbye, and one commissar started yelling at them rudely, something about landowners, bloodsuckers, and so forth. Inside the house there were loud and unfamiliar voices, the sound of doors slam-ming, laughter, it got entirely unbearable and we were happy when finally the cart came. . . . When we sat down and took off, the whole crowd removed their hats and stood bowing, crossing themselves, and wailing."

The Farming Classes

The drive to collectivize Russian farming did not succeed completely. In rural areas, tension remained between loyal Communists and those who resisted, either openly or secretly, the new state and its economic system. In addition, the state allowed rural families to keep small, private plots of land, which always drew more care and cultivation than collectively owned farmland. The traditional class divisions among Russian farmers continued in force, expressed in the terms described by Serge Schmemann in his book *Echoes of a Native Land*:

> Poor peasants, bednyaki, were defined as those who owned virtually nothing. Next up the ladder of socialist worthiness were the srednyaki, who might have a horse and a couple of cows. Anyone who had more, and especially anyone who used hired labor, was a kulak, an exploiter and sworn enemy of the known order. Needless to say, the bednyak was usually the laziest and most drunken of the villagers, while anyone who resisted Soviet power was by definition a kulak.[15]

In general, kulaks were those independent or successful farmers who resisted collectivization. For the Communist government, the term became synonymous with "outlaw" or "criminal." Many kulaks were arrested and executed or sent into exile along with other political prisoners. Others were allowed to leave the collective farms but could not bring away any equipment or livestock, all of which was considered state property. These kulaks worked small parcels of land that were doled out to them by the state. But they also paid heavy taxes that made it impossible for most to survive on their own.

The forced collectivization of Russian farms had long-lasting effects that were felt every day by people living in the countryside. The execution or imprisonment of millions of peasants brought about a nationwide shortage of labor. Once they became state property, many fields that had once been well tended went uncultivated and reverted to fallow cropland. State-owned heavy equipment, such as trucks and tractors, often broke down. The distribution of goods proved even worse in rural areas than in the cities. Russian villagers

Forced collectivization on Russian farms did not succeed completely.

often could not find staple goods such as bread, flour, and milk in their shops.

In his book *Lenin's Tomb*, author David Remnick describes the effects of collectivization in Russia's Vologda region:

> There were more than seven thousand "ruined" villages, ghost towns of collapsing houses and untended land that had once been working farms. For decades, the young had been abandoning the wasted village in droves, searching for a decent wage in the textile and machine-tool plants of Vologda. Like others before them, their search for the industrial utopia turned out to be fruitless. They found only miserable work in textile plants and lived in vast dormitories.[16]

Life on the Collective

The Russian kolkhoz, or collective farm, was a self-contained community with its own stores, small businesses, schools, museums, recreational facilities, and cinemas. Many of these collectives covered hundreds of square miles and counted thousands of families as members. The Communist government saw the big, modern kolkhoz as a replacement for the traditional small and backward village, and it partially succeeded—thousands of Russian villages disappeared completely under communism.

Russian families living on a kolkhoz commonly owned their homes and rented the land they worked. To manage the business of the collective, they elected committees. Members of the committees set planting and harvest schedules, doled out land and equipment, passed decrees on working hours and holidays, and meted out punishment and rewards as they saw fit. They set production quotas, harvesting schedules, and delivery dates based on a plan passed by a regional government, which received its instructions in turn from the central government in Moscow. The collective committee paid wages to individual farmers and workers out of the collective's central treasury. Wages sometimes included grain and feed for the animals owned by individual families.

Through proclamations and public meetings, the boards and chairpersons of the collective farms exhorted their members to work harder and produce more. The state viewed meeting or exceeding production quotas as a mark of loyalty to the revolution and the ongoing struggle to achieve communism. It rewarded valiant effort with bonuses in the form of higher wages, better equipment, and honorable mention in local newspapers. Occasionally, the committees waged campaigns to serve civic purposes or to deal with certain problems. According to one description,

> "Bread for the motherland," a campaign against wasting bread, and another [to] help prevent brush fires by discouraging smoking in the fields, are waged through colorful roadside slogans. The cornfield is a battlefield in the onward march towards communism. Everywhere the responsible citizen is exhorted to fulfill his socialist obligations—to be a diligent worker and a vigilant patriot.[17]

According to Soviet law, collective farms had to sell all of their livestock and harvest to the state, which paid fixed prices for produce whether it came from the collective or from the individual. In practice, the prices paid often did not cover the costs of buying and maintaining equipment, any extra labor that had to be hired at busy times of the year, or the many other incidental expenses. As a result, many

The Urban Effect

Under Joseph Stalin, Communist Russia went through a drastic transformation. New factories and new cities, and forced collectivization, drew millions of rural families off their land. The nation's leaders wanted industrialization to bring Russia to a living standard equal to that of Western European countries. But one result of this change—a greater demand for material goods and personal freedom—was not foreseen by Russia's leaders. These demands, in the end, played an important role in the downfall of communism. In *The New Russians*, published in 1990 just before the fall of communism, author Hedrick Smith summarizes this "urban effect."

"At the end of World War II, only 56.1 million people lived in cities; by 1987, that figure had more than tripled to 180 million. In Khrushchev's time [1955–1964], there were only three cities with a population of more than 1 million; in 1980, there were twenty-three. That massive shift from country to city has slowly worn away the peasant mentality that long characterized the Russian narod, or masses. In the early 1970s, this peasant mentality had been a prime source of the political passivity and fatalism of many Russians.

But during my recent travels, one provincial leader after another complained to me that large numbers of young people, especially those with some education and skills, had left dreary villages for big cities in search of better jobs, housing, clothes, stimulation—the latest movies, rock music. Such middle-class urges now made these younger urban transplants dissatisfied with the old, ossified ways of doing things; they were susceptible to the promise of change, impatient and ready to lash back when reforms failed to deliver a better life."

collectives operated at a loss. To make up the loss, the collectives often diverted their produce to merchants in Russian towns and cities where the state still allowed street markets to operate.

In addition to the disastrous effects of central planning, the collective farms had to contend with Mother Nature. In most arable regions of Russia, the principal crop was wheat, which demands fertile soil and regular rainfall. Since these conditions did not always hold, harvests were sometimes poor. Since the state could not always provide food and basic goods when needed, the collective often had to depend on its own stores to feed its members.

Another serious problem facing collective managers was mechanical: Essential farm machinery often ran poorly or not at all. Tractors and combines were plentiful throughout Communist Russia, where the state held up such items as important symbols of the country's progress and modernization. Since heavy equipment belonged to the collective, however, no one took a personal interest in keeping it in good repair. Spare parts proved hard to obtain, and shortages of fuel often kept the tractors idle. Many skilled operators left the collective in search of better-paid work in the city, leaving behind older or untrained individuals to cope with the complex machinery as best they could.

The result of the system was a great waste of Russia's vast agricultural resources. As Michael Dobbs relates,

One-third of the food harvest was lost because of inadequate storage facilities, an outdated transportation system, and general mechanical failures. Tractors and combine harvesters left factories in such poor condition that they invariably had to be repaired as soon as they arrived on the farm.[18]

Private Plots

Although all land in Communist Russia belonged to the state, farmers in the countryside had always considered the land adjoining their own houses to belong to them. Recognizing that the collectivization of every inch of land posed an impossible task, the state allowed each family its private plot, limiting the size to half a hectare. The farmers could put this land to any purpose they saw fit. They could build small sheds for the storage of tools or fuel, raise a few chickens, keep a horse or a cow, or tend small gardens of potatoes, cabbages, beets, and other vegetables.

Most farmers gave higher priority to their tiny but private plots, which could be tended without the use of tractors. Owners could trade the produce of their plots to the collective in exchange for grain or animal feed. In theory, farmers could also sell their own produce to the state. In practice, they did not, because the state's prices were too low. Instead, most farmers sold their private produce at public markets, which convened in Russian towns and cities once or twice a week. At the markets, sellers could charge whatever prices they wanted for their goods. Although prices were higher, the public crowded the farmers' markets because the quality was better. As one writer describes the Russian street market,

Fruit, vegetables and meat generally have a better flavor and are more varied here than in the State shops. But the prices are not fixed, and are therefore high, sometimes even astronomical. The average Soviet citizen goes to the kolkhoz market only under exceptional circumstances, otherwise his budget would never suffice. Besides veal from their calves and potatoes from their allotments, the kolkhozniki also sell produce which they have picked—berries or mushrooms from the forests. In the early morning you can see these robust women arrive from their fields, often a long way away, hire a stall, put on the compulsory white apron and sleeves, and spread out their modest riches.[19]

Small private garden plots allowed under the Communist system provided farmers the opportunity to sell their produce in the public market.

For millions of Russians in the countryside, private plots made the difference between comfort and poverty. But these plots also harmed the operations of the collective. Farmers who kept themselves busy planting, weeding, and harvesting their own food gave little attention to poorly paid work on collective land. Although the state rewarded productive workers with citations, medals, and small bonuses, most farmers preferred the straightforward profits offered by selling their own food at their own price.

The Hunter's Life

There was more than one way to make a living off the land in Communist Russia. Siberia, the vast range of forest and tundra that stretched across northern Russia, was home to a large population of licensed professional hunters. Professional hunters were expected to supply a certain quota of hides and meat to the state each year, at fixed prices. Hunters earned money for furs and animal skins and were given a small bounty by the state for each wolf skin. (In some rural areas of Russia, wolves still presented a danger to livestock and children.)

In many parts of Siberia, hunting was the most common occupation. Professional hunters typically lived in isolated homes or shacks located near a stream or lake. They spent their days tracking game and laying traps, moving when necessary to a new region when the natural stock of deer, elk, moose, fox, and other game grew too sparse to support them. Even in the vast reaches of Siberia, natural and mineral resources were limited, and most Russian hunters, timber cutters, and miners took no interest in environmentalism or in husbanding land and resources. The state did little to encourage conservation, as it placed a much higher priority on setting and meeting production quotas.

Poaching among unlicensed hunters, and on land considered off limits to hunting, was a common activity. In search of antlers or hides that could be sold on the black market, or meat that could be sold for a clear profit in nearby villages, poachers killed entire herds of elk and deer that ranged on public nature preserves. Poaching had a long tradition in Russia; in tsarist days, unlicensed hunters had tramped through private lands while using leg traps and rifles to bag their game. Modern poachers employed more efficient and destructive methods, such as firing machine guns from trucks or motorcycles. Communist-era poachers also used helicopters, snowmobiles, and motorboats.

Moving to the City

Hunters as well as farmers knew that the best living in Communist Russia could be had in the cities. As a result, emigration from rural areas brought a constant and acute labor shortage to many Russian collectives. Many young Russians could not resist the lure of an easier livelihood and the sheer abundance of the city, as compared to life on the kolkhoz. One writer describes the effect of arriving in Moscow after spending time in the countryside:

Entering Moscow by road after driving along bumpy, potholed roads crowded with lopsided trucks and buses and lined by rows of villages that had no running water leaves an indelible impression. The roads and streets suddenly widen and become smoother. Even on the outskirts, tall apartment houses, broad avenues, the heavy flow of traffic, shiny cars and brightly lit stores convey a sense of "civilization," of a glossy, elegant, lively, vibrant metropolis. Such trips vicariously gave me the peasant's point of view. I began to understand why hundreds of thousands of them stream into Moscow each day to shop. . . . I started to understand why the platforms of the Byelorussian, Kiev, Kazan, and Yaroslavl railway stations in Moscow are inevitably crowded with masses of peasants lugging huge baskets of eggs, canned goods and sweets or whatever else happens to be in short supply in their villages.[20]

Yet it was not only the urge to have a better life that prompted mass emigration to the cities. The collectivization effort of the 1930s had forced millions of farmers off the land, and the devastation of World War II that followed also depopulated the countryside. There was also a movement of workers from the western regions of Russia to Siberia. Although conditions were harsh in the northern forests and tundra, mining and timber jobs offered much higher wages as compensation for the cold and isolation. Anything, it seemed, was better than agricultural work and life on the Russian collective.

Labor shortages were particularly bad at harvest time. In late summer and fall, local committees issued urgent calls for help. Every Russian student and worker, no matter what their status or what they did for a living, experienced these fall harvest campaigns. They boarded trucks that brought them out to the countryside to dig potatoes or beets—root crops that could not be easily harvested by heavy machinery.

Ironically, one factor contributing to the shortage of rural labor was the state's emphasis on universal and compulsory education. The new schools operating on the collectives allowed many rural Russians to achieve higher levels of literacy and technical skill. This also meant that many young men and women who at one time would have stayed on the land chose instead to move to the city, where they could find better paid work in urban factories. The citizens of Communist Russia realized that a good education represented the key to whatever success and independence the state would allow them.

Life in Fedorovsky

For many Russians, living conditions did not improve with the establishment of the collective farm. Thousands of small villages, each with a single street dividing a row of wooden houses made of sawn timber or logs, still dotted the map of western and southern Russia. Many remained impoverished and isolated, without electricity, telephones, or indoor plumbing. Kevin Klose in his book *Russia and the Russians* gives the following view of Fedorovsky, a village lying just 250 miles west of Moscow.

"Contact barely existed beyond the horizon of the hamlet. In spring and fall, the land became a quagmire of flooded streams, rutted rural paths, and fields sunk in water. Thatch roofs leaked, backyards disintegrated into muddy wallows. Mud was everywhere. Travel was impossible. In winter, storms raged and howled across the broad countryside, obliterating such signposts as there were; families stayed indoors for days on end, stirring only to dig for potatoes or turnips from root cellars, gather firewood, and feed their emaciated cattle."

Education

The founders of the Soviet Union considered education one of the most important functions of the state. The teaching of the young, from the moment they first set foot in a school, was designed to make them into patriotic and loyal citizens. The proper books and articles, created by state-approved writers, would guard them against the influence of communism's many enemies, both at home and abroad. Memorizing slogans favorable to Lenin and his works would inspire them to carry on his revolution—always an unfinished business—in their homes and in their future places of work.

Lenin and his successors required that all children attend school. They also made universal literacy a key goal of the Communist state. As a result, the revolution opened up new opportunities and avenues of expression for millions of people. Education allowed the sons and daughters of farmers and ordinary laborers a place in society they could not have achieved before 1917. Writer Andrei Sinyavsky summed up these achievements:

> Initially there was a wholesale awakening of people's creative energy, the various manifestations of which made up the panorama of the real-life utopia. Yesterday a herdsman, today the commander of a regiment or an army; in some sense this too was an actual utopia. Yesterday a tailor, today a commissar. Yesterday illiterate, today a halting reader of Pravda who understands everything.[21]

The Communist government did succeed in a dramatic expansion of literacy. Before the Communists came to power, less than half of the population of Russia could read. By 1939, 81 percent of the country was literate, and by the 1980s, literacy had reached 95 percent. Most Russian students were also quite knowledgeable in their chosen field of study.

Younger students learned the outline of Russia's past filtered through the views of Communist thinkers and writers. Behind the study of reading and history lay a more important goal: instilling the desired attitude toward the state and its philosophy. Russian students were told, repeatedly, about the virtues and achievements of the Communist regime. Instructors, following directives from the Soviet education ministry, proclaimed communism the best system in the world, one that guaranteed workers a job and a decent standard of living. Capitalism, on the other hand, was portrayed as a system that forced laborers to toil in an indifferent society in which unemployment, poverty, crime, and other social ills ran rampant.

Under Stalin, the Communist Party had decided to reward itself with a uniform and laudatory history, as writer David Remnick explains:

> In 1934, the Communist Party Central Committee issued a decree calling for a strict ideological version of history to become doctrine in all textbooks, schools, universities, and institutes. Stalin himself supervised the writing and publication in

a run of fifty million copies of the famous Short Course, an angry ideological tract that was, in the words of historian Genrikh Joffe, "like a hammer pounding nails of falsehood into every schoolboy's and schoolgirl's brain." The Short Course was a textbook of determinist history with all events leading, necessarily, inexorably, to a glorious conclusion: the rightness and might of the present regime. . . . An entire people's understanding of themselves was meant to dwell within this text. To question or defy the dogma was to admit guilt before the criminal code.[22]

The Education System

A national ministry, the People's Commissariat for Education, was responsible for all teaching in Communist Russian schools. (The state did not allow private or parochial schools, but certain specialized schools were reserved for sons and daughters of the party elite, and many taught in English or French.) The ministry established the correct teaching methods and materials, to be used in a uniform manner from one end of the country to the other. It decided the subjects to cover, and the time of year and the order in which instructors would cover them. It approved new teachers and assigned them to schools and class levels. It awarded good performance, both by students and teachers, and punished disobedience and disloyalty.

The education ministry was a political instrument, serving to indoctrinate society's youngest members with the policies and outlook of the regime in power. After basic literacy and Communist ideology, education focused on scientific and technical training. Students learned practical skills to be applied

Soviet schoolchildren were constantly indoctrinated in Communist dogma.

in their future occupations, whether in a factory, on a collective farm, or in a hospital or research institute. The ultimate goal of all such training was to turn the mass of unskilled laborers into a population of skilled workers. In theory, this would advance the national economy and put Russia on an equal footing with the rest of the modern world.

A Day in School

Russian children began attending preschool nurseries at the age of three or four. Within the classroom, teachers and guardians did not yet expose these youngest students to academic subjects. But the students did learn much about the society they lived in and the government they had. Yelena Khanga, whose grandparents moved from Mississippi to Russia in the 1920s, recalled:

In the view of Russian educators, premature emphasis on academic instruction robs children of their childhood. But no child was ever too young for political education. Each of my nursery classrooms featured a small shrine to Lenin, consisting of a portrait surrounded by ribbons and fresh flowers. We children vied for the honor of bringing flowers and placing them on a small table underneath the picture; in this way, we were prepared for the more direct political education we would receive in elementary school.[23]

Formal school began at age seven for most children in Communist Russia. Primary students studied the Russian language and literature, mathematics, art, and music. The curriculum also included daily physical education classes. By the third grade (age

First Debates

Schoolchildren in Communist Russia learned at a young age that politics and political argument would make up an important part of their lives. Politics grew especially intense when encountering foreigners from Western countries. As quoted in *An American Family in Moscow*, by Leona and Jerrold Schechter, one young American named Stevo learned quickly that his own society would come under intense scrutiny and criticism.

"It was during the first year that I had my first political argument. I was on dezhurstvo (cleanup) duty with my deskmate. It was our turn to clean up the classroom after school. We picked up the trash on the floor, mopped it, emptied the trash, washed the board, and watered the flowers. The girl doing it with me called me a 'little capitalist' because I wasn't very good at sweeping and mopping. She said that I had always had maids to do the work for me. She was right, but I argued violently that it wasn't true. I became very able with a broom and mop from that day on. She talked on and on, citing America's outstanding faults: the Vietnam war, racism, poverty, and class differences. 'JFK was the only good American president you ever had,' she said. I told her he was a very rich capitalist and exploited a lot of workers, but she wouldn't believe me. We were both eleven years old."

nine) students also were studying foreign languages. The state required that all students attend school through the tenth grade. After the eighth grade, students could choose to stay in the same school or attend a vocational school to learn a trade. In secondary school, students studied mathematics, languages, history, and science, including physics, chemistry, and biology.

The school day began at 8:00 in the morning. After reaching their school on foot or by public transportation, the uniformed students lined up on the school grounds or in the courtyard. At the sound of the first bell, they followed their teachers into the classroom. The youngest students attended school until noon, the rest until 2:00 in the afternoon.

Within the classroom, teaching depended largely on memorization and rote learning— the repetition of key phrases and concepts learned from the instructor. Students memorized correct answers, while teachers emphasized skill and practice at public speaking, rather than writing ability. To answer questions or to give recitations, students stood up and faced their instructors, with their peers listening. During examinations, teachers posed essay or exam problems to the student, who was required to answer the problems orally.

Grades for classroom work and examinations ran from 1 to 5, with 5 being the top score and 1 the lowest. Students earned marks every day they attended school. Consistent good marks assured the student a chance at entering a university, which in turn promised a prestigious and well-paid professional career.

In the 1980s, Russian schools went through a reform that was supposed to allow more liberty in subject matter and teaching methods. Nevertheless, the old ways died hard. Writer Adam Hochschild attended a class for students talented in physics and mathematics. The subject of the class was the regime of Joseph Stalin. Hochschild writes,

> The homework for the class period I sat in on had been to study a booklet of readings. Even though there were less than half a dozen of them, the students sat in a row facing the teacher, who remained behind a desk. One after another, each student, looking stiff and anxious, spoke for ten minutes or so in a rapid monotone, summarizing the main points of an article from the booklet. "Svetlov says . . . Svetlov says . . . Svetlov thinks that there are four reasons for . . ." Then the student stopped, relieved, and another boy or girl carried on: "Borisov says . . . Borisov says . . . Borisov names three factors leading to . . ."[24]

The Young Pioneers and the Komsomol

Many students in Communist Russia joined the Young Pioneers, an organization for boys and girls between the ages of nine and fourteen. A red kerchief worn around the neck marked a Russian youngster as a member of the Pioneers. New members received a copy of *Our Very Best Friend*, a book about Lenin. At meetings, they heard lectures on the history of Lenin and on the revolution. They sang revolutionary songs and reviewed required books and articles on the history and philosophy of communism. During their summer vacations, the members of the Pioneers spent a month in camps scattered throughout the Russian countryside. Their behavior and their attitude remained under close scrutiny by Young Pioneers guides, leaders who gave words of praise for outstanding achievements but held up to criticism any member's failure in duties or loyalty to the party.

Above all, the Young Pioneers instilled a sense of civic duty and a collective spirit, attributes befitting future adult members of the Communist Party. Young Pioneers saw their membership in a party organization as a vital ingredient in their classroom work, their relations with others, and their everyday life. In the 1980s, a former Young Pioneer named Rita Tikhonova described her Pioneers experience as follows:

> It's stayed as something sacred for me! Taking part makes you feel so responsible. While the State is large-scale government, the school was managed by us, governed by us. We decided who should be on duty at school on any given day, and what we would do after lessons were over. We decided everything ourselves. We believed in what we were doing so sincerely, we did it with our heart and soul.[25]

At the age of fourteen, children were eligible for membership in the Komsomol, or Young Communist League, which accepted members up to the age of twenty-nine. The Komsomol had its own party newspaper, *Komsomolskaya Pravda*, as well as its own sports and cultural organizations. There were Komsomol offices in every Russian city, and the Komsomol included an entire committee organization of its own—a socialist government in miniature.

Komsomol membership marked the young Soviet citizen as a promising member of the revolutionary elite. It was virtually a requirement for admittance to a university. Students quickly learned that Komsomol and Communist Party membership offered them more opportunities for good jobs, for higher education, and for foreign travel.

But Komsomol membership also brought a close examination of one's academic performance, political views, and personal life. Komsomol members had few secrets, as each individual was expected to closely follow and report on the actions of the others. Those

Komsomol members march as tourists look on.

A College Education

A college education in Communist Russia did not always produce happy, optimistic students. In the early 1970s John Dornberg, author of *The New Tsars: Russia Under Stalin's Heirs*, recorded one university student's grim assessment of his future,

"'Here it isn't what but who you know,' he said. 'No matter how good an engineer I turn out to be, I won't get anywhere unless I join the party. That's where careers are made and they are all hypocrites.

'I can tell you now what my future is going to look like. Ten years after graduation I'll have a two-room flat, some flimsy furniture, maybe a refrigerator, a television set that will have cost me two to three months' salary, a one-room hut in the country which I'll call a dacha, and perhaps, if I have been lucky, very lucky, an old car. . . .

'Sure, I'm studying English. But where will I ever use it? Certainly not to travel abroad. That is beyond my wildest dreams—unless I were to join the party and become a careerist. That's not exactly my idea of living, either. So, for what I'm eventually going to get, why should I knock myself out?'"

having problems at school or trouble with the law or their parents would find themselves summoned by a Komsomol officer to be counseled and, if necessary, warned.

Komsomol members followed the basic Communist ideal of living and working collectively, in the most democratic manner possible. Komsomol committees imitated the soviets of adults, and some Komsomol organizations even held authority within Russia's schools. One person interviewed by author Joan Hasler recalls Komsomol procedure:

There was a meeting of the Komsomol Committee held at our school at which we decided to re-organise our school life. The suggestions was to have self-management at our school. The idea was met with great enthusiasm. A plan of rules was worked out according to which all important matters must be decided by the General Meeting attended by all the pupils except the juniors [youngest students], and all the teachers. This meeting elects a School-managing Council. In all its activities the Council is accountable to the Meeting. The Meeting elects an Inspection Committee which checks up on whether the decisions of the Meeting are being carried out. In between the meetings the entire school management, including the disposal of the finances, is in the hands of the Council. At school there is also a Teacher's Council. If it thinks the decision of the Meeting is wrong it can cancel it within five days after it has been made, provided it furnishes convincing arguments.[26]

University Studies

To qualify for entrance to a university, applicants had to have a high school diploma and pass a difficult series of entrance examinations. Their scores on the examinations decided their placement. Admissions committees also considered practical experience and gave preference to students having a background of work considered useful. The most competitive and

Universities favored the applications from the sons and daughters of workers as it aided the national effort to eliminate social distinctions.

prestigious universities in the country were those in Moscow and Leningrad. (In fact; the main building of Moscow University was the largest single building in the capital.) Membership in the Komsomol also proved crucial in earning a place at a desired school.

Another important ingredient for university admission was one's social origins. Applications from the sons and daughters of workers were favored. Early in Communist Russia's history, schools usually turned away members of the "bourgeois" (middle) classes as well as intellectuals—writers, artists, and all others who didn't get their hands dirty while earning a living. This was part of the national effort to level Russian society and eliminate social distinctions (other than the distinction of party membership). As a result, the children of Russian workers soon arrived at highly paid and responsible positions, as well as the highest ranks of the Communist Party itself.

For Russian students, university studies lasted from four to six years. At the highest levels, teaching under the Communist regime was extremely specialized. Future engineers and doctors, for example, received training only in their field of study. The state made no effort to broaden their education and produce a graduate who was knowledgeable in a variety of different subjects. Within the humanities, the topic of Marxism-Leninism prevailed. The state did not deem any other system of philosophy worthy of study, unless to point out its faults and shortcomings.

University students had to arrange their own living quarters, as there were no dormitories available. Rather than paying tuition, students received a monthly stipend from the state, which was supposed to cover their basic expenses. Once the courses were completed, the state assigned graduates jobs in their chosen field. Typically, graduates had to remain in this profession for a minimum of two years. Many of those destined for careers as writers, for example, were first assigned reporting jobs at small-town newspapers for the sake of practical experience.

Students

Despite the availability to many of college educations, as well as guaranteed job placement for graduates, students were often restless. Especially in the 1950s and 1960s, when Communist Russia reached a higher standard of living than had been possible earlier, and citizens were allowed more contact with the outside world, young people began to rebel against the system. When they could, Russian teenagers bought and traded records and cassette tapes of Western rock bands banned by their government. They also coveted T-shirts, especially those printed in English, and any article of clothing carrying a designer label.

Above all, young Russians sought a pair of blue jeans, which became the ultimate symbol of protest against the state and the system. The origins of their blue jeans even divided students into distinct social classes: The upper crust wore Lee, Wrangler, and Levi's; the middle class wore jeans from the rest of Europe; and the lowest class could afford only the cheapest kind, those made in the Soviet Union.

In Communist Russia, blue jeans came to stand for something much more important than fashion: the concepts of freedom and affluence, ideas considered irrelevant and dangerous in the official Communist system. The fad for blue jeans reached from the schools and universities to all levels of a still-diverse Russian society, from professionals to servants. As David K. Shipler relates,

Educational Experience

The work detail was a part of ordinary life for Russian students living under the Communist system. The state requisitioned the labor of workers as well as students when harvests came in or when special civic projects were under way. Attendance was mandatory, as writer Yuri Tarnopolsky remembers in *Memoirs of 1984.*

"When I was a student, we were forced to work every summer for at least a month in the fields. At least once a year we were ordered to come to the school with a travel bag, aluminum mug, spoon, some food, clothes, and the famous Russian high boots so indispensable in the countryside's chronic mud.

We would be taken to the railway station, put into freight cars, and transported over several hundred miles to the farmlands. After unloading, we were stuffed into large open pickups designed to carry grain and other agricultural loads, which shook the hell out of us on the terrible dirt roads. . . .

We harvested corn from dawn to dusk. I was so exhausted that I could fall asleep while standing upright and wake up when my knees bent. We did not have a shower for a month. It was the late sixties, and Stalin was dead. It was a party order, and party orders could not be discussed. . . .

Every fall, after the first frost, we had to pick potatoes from the loosened soil with our bare hands, pack them into hundred-pound bags, and load them into a pickup. Gloves were very hard to find in the stores, so if I had a pair, it was certainly not for potatoes. It was in the seventies, after Khrushchev had been demoted and Brezhnev had come to power. It was a party order, and our dear party never made mistakes."

A friend of mine whose parents were both medical professors told me that at her sister's fifteenth birthday party, all the boys and girls, who clustered separately, wore American jeans—every one of them. At a prestigious Moscow architectural institute's annual dance the students one year built a huge model of a pair of dungarees to tower over the dance floor—the centerpiece of their decorations and a totem to the idolatry of their age. An American woman shocked her Russian maid by removing and throwing away a leather Lee patch that was coming loose from a pair of jeans. The patch was the whole idea, the maid said, and snapped it up to sew on a pair of her son's.[27]

But Russian students also took care to not go too far in defying the system. Their dress, behavior, and expressed opinions were under the watchful attention of teachers and fellow students. Their peers always had the weapon of public humiliation to use against those who got out of line. According to Joan Hasler in *The Making of Russia*,

> Students discuss and pronounce upon any failings of their fellows, whether idleness or antisocial behavior. The teachers in one Moscow school assured us that this was all that was necessary to ensure attentive and well-behaved pupils; they said there were no discipline problems in any school in Russia, just as they said there were no left-handed children—it's just a matter of training![28]

The basic goal of all the rules and regulations was to prepare the student to take his or her place as an obedient and productive member of society. In Communist Russia, adult citizens' most important identities were as workers, and it was as a worker that each person would be measured by the state and by other Soviet citizens.

Work in Communist Russia

The leaders of Russia's Communist revolution proclaimed their ideas and actions in the name of the workers. By "workers," Marx, Lenin, and their followers meant the masses of industrial laborers who worked for low wages and for the benefit of factory owners and, in turn, the capitalist governments. It was for the workers that the revolution was made, and it was for the workers that the Soviet government, according to its own propaganda, had abolished the unjust and corrupt system of capitalism and had replaced it with a society modeled on socialist principles.

Many workers did see their conditions improve after the revolution. Others believed that the sacrifices they made were worth the ultimate goal: a Communist utopia. Nikita Khrushchev, the Soviet leader of the 1950s and early 1960s, had suffered great privations as a young coal miner. But as he wrote in his memoirs, *Khrushchev Remembers,*

> Most of us willingly submitted to privation because, as we saw it, we had to squeeze the last drop of productivity out of our resources in order to industrialize the country as quickly as possible. If we were to survive, we had to catch up with the capitalists. Sometimes achieving this goal required sacrificing moral principles as well as material comfort. But on the whole the people gladly underwent these sufferings for the Party's sake. And in the space of a few years we brought a modern industrial society into being.[29]

In Communist Russia, the ordinary factory worker was transformed into a national icon. Posters and paintings depicted steelworkers, mechanics, assemblers, and their colleagues as mighty heroes, achieving incredible feats of productivity and wielding the tools of their trade in triumph. The state considered the subject of labor to be the most fit for plays, films, and operas; works exploring individual human experience and emotion were considered

The worker was glorified in Communist Russia as depicted on this poster.

The Legendary Stakhanov

During the 1930s, Russia was caught up in a feverish campaign of industrialization and economic growth. In his book *Russia and the Russians*, author Kevin Klose describes the rise of the "shock worker."

"The shock-worker phenomenon arose in the Donbas in 1935, when an obscure miner named Alexei Stakhanov claimed that he had singlehandedly produced 102 tons of coal in a single six-hour shift, more than fifteen times the average seven tons per work per shift. Within weeks, Stakhanovite madness swept the coalfields as mine after mine arranged competitions to win the favor of the tyrant Stalin. Record setters were hailed as heroes, but underachievers faced reprisals, which could take many forms. At the least, they could be docked pay or denied bonuses they had easily qualified for in earlier times. At the worst, thousands were sent into the rapidly expanding concentration camps of northeastern Siberia on phony charges of 'sabotage' and 'wrecking.'

Miners [in reaction] fled the coalfields. Stakhanovites were murdered. The insanity finally burned out toward the end of the decade. Many years later, after Stalin was denounced, Stakhanov's original production claims were proved to be fraudulent."

"decadent." Writers and poets hailed the factory worker as the man, or woman, of the future. From their ranks would come the Russian leaders of tomorrow; their class would rise as a new aristocracy, guiding the nation while overcoming the poverty and prejudices of the past.

The revolution did, in fact, transform the day-to-day reality of the Russian workplace. But Russian workers found that under Communist rule, they had exchanged one sort of brutal and exhausting routine for another. They also found that Communist bosses could crack the whip as mercilessly as their capitalist counterparts. Although the worker and the worker's family gained some comfort and prosperity, as compared to the prerevolutionary past, it came at great cost to the individual and to the nation as a whole.

Working in the Quota System

In the 1920s, the Soviet government began drawing up five-year economic plans, which formed the impetus for all work carried out in Russia and the other Soviet republics. These five-year plans set down production quotas in every sector of the economy, from tractors and automobiles to machinery, clothing, steel, furniture, ball bearings, cement, coal, and chemicals. The plans paid no attention to consumer demand, to the cost of supplying and transporting raw materials, or to the availability of workers. Nevertheless, they were supposed to constitute a scientific and logical method, free of the unpredictability and risk of the free-market system. The state gave the highest priority to military supplies and heavy industry in an effort to keep up with the modernizing capitalist nations of Western Europe.

The commissars of each industry handed down the production quotas to individual factory managers. There was no competition with other factories producing the same goods, and there were few guidelines controlling the quality of the goods. The planners told the factories the quantity of goods to produce, the amount of raw materials to order and from whom to order them, the prices to charge for finished goods, the total wages to pay, and the number of workers to hire. In turn, the managers told their workers to fulfill a certain quota of items to be manufactured in a certain amount of time. Car factories were to turn out a certain number of new cars each month. Bakeries would produce a set number of fresh loaves every day. Miners were to dig a certain tonnage of coal. Trains were to carry a certain number of passengers and be driven a certain distance.

If the quota was surpassed, the worker or workers responsible, in theory, would earn a salary bonus. Workers who distinguished themselves often enough might see their face on a poster that praised their achievements. Newspapers and magazines might write glowing articles on factories or mines that surpassed their quotas.

On the other hand, failure to meet the quota resulted in punishment. Managers might deliver a stern reprimand at a company-wide meeting. Scheduled salary raises might be canceled. Certain privileges granted to the workers, such as vacations, might be suspended or taken away entirely.

The system of quotas often brought about a frantic rush toward the end of the month in order to meet the state's production target. If possible, the buying public avoided products made toward the end of the month, when quality-control standards were all but abandoned. However, goods produced at any time of the month were often shoddy, and since in the planned economy prices were generally affordable, broken items were often discarded instead of repaired. In addition, there was no incentive for innovation, for producing new products, or for making old products in a new,

A bakery worker checks loaves of fresh bread. All kinds of factory workers had to meet quotas for the production of goods.

more efficient way. For workers, for managers, and for their state-owned companies, there was no fear of failure and no profit motive.

At all stages, laborers were reminded that they were working not for individual rewards but for a common goal: the achievement of communism and the advance of Russia to the front rank of industrialized nations. Propaganda in the form of posters and banners proclaimed these motives in schools, offices, and workplaces of all kinds, alongside posters of Lenin and, beginning in the 1930s, of Stalin. In every factory, management held classes and lectures for the workers to remind them of these principles and to reinforce their loyalty to the state. Stirring slogans such as "Workers of the World Unite!" were carried over from revolutionary days, when a principal function of the Communist Party was the education and indoctrination of a largely illiterate population.

The Workers' Paradise: In Theory

In theory, communism provided a job for every worker. Work was said to be the highest civic duty of the citizen, and those who did not work were shunned as parasites. The state considered quitting work a criminal offense until 1956, the year that voluntary resignations

Working at the Top

Working conditions could be hard for people in Communist Russia, despite daily reminders that they were laboring for a common good. Life was a little better for the apparatchiks, members of the Communist Party with jobs in government agencies and planning bureaus. Although Russia was supposed to be a classless society, the progress of apparatchiks up the professional ladder was marked by hundreds of small details and privileges. Journalist Michael Dobbs, in *Down with Big Brother*, describes a few of these telltale signs.

"In the Communist utopia created by the apparatchiks for their own benefit, every rung on the bureaucratic ladder had its own special privileges and rewards. Dachas, medals, clothing allowances, and even cemetery lots all were distributed according to a Byzantine table of ranks. Instructors had the right to a new fur hat once every two years, while secretaries and drivers were limited to one every three years. A visitor could tell where power lay in the Central Committee by following the carpet runner in the hallway. It glided past the offices of ordinary apparatchiks but made right-angle detours into the suites of the top leaders. Another telltale sign was the portraits of the Communist deities. When a bureaucrat reached the rank of deputy head of department, he was automatically allocated a portrait of Marx instead of the standard portrait of Lenin. Heads of department had large portraits of both Marx and Lenin on their walls. Then there was the question of how tea was served. A lower-ranking official was served tea on a plain tray. Once he reached the rank of chief of sector, the tray suddenly sprouted a napkin. In apparatchik-speak, the promotion was referred to as 'receiving the napkin.'"

became legal. In case a worker did lose his or her position, the authorities allowed four months to find a new job. After an additional month of unemployment, the jobless were liable to arrest.

The law granted Russian workers certain benefits, including paid vacation and paid sick leave. If a worker was injured and disabled on the job, he or she had the right to a disability pension and retraining. Pregnant women were allowed sixteen weeks of maternity leave, and a further three months off without pay, after which the law obliged their employers to rehire them. On retirement, workers were entitled to a pension of between 50 and 100 percent of their maximum annual salary. The normal retirement age was sixty for men, fifty-five for women.

The Workers' Paradise: In Practice

Soviet law granted double wages to those working overtime, but often these wages were not paid, as salaries were handed out at the discretion of the factory managers. In place of extra pay, bosses sometimes granted extra time off from work. In many factories, bonuses for high production or overtime were only paid to party members. Loyalty to the party was rewarded by better tools, higher wages, or better apartments. But those who complained about pay or working conditions could find themselves receiving no paid overtime, assigned the most unpleasant or dangerous tasks, or even summarily fired. Labor unions offered little help to individuals with grievances, and strikes never took place.

Thus, it is not surprising that absenteeism ran high in Russian factories. Workers often took time off to stand in line for goods on sale or to attend to other personal business. If an idler or absentee stopped showing up for work altogether, the managers often kept him or her on the list of employees, a practice that allowed them to draw absentees' salaries for their own accounts. Labor laws made it nearly impossible to fire a chronically late or incompetent worker, and as a result, Soviet factories were often overstaffed with nonessential employees.

Russian factories were run inefficiently and wastefully. Since work property—tools, uniforms, workbenches, assembly lines, lighting fixtures, generators, and so on—belonged to the state, few bothered to maintain such property or to repair it when it broke down. Workers and their bosses allowed materials to deteriorate and left expensive machinery to rust outdoors, unguarded and unmoved, exposed to the rain and the harsh Russian winters. The result was a tremendous loss of machinery, raw materials, and other productive property throughout the country.

Another result of this disregard for state property was the theft of factory goods, by managers as well as workers. Tools and other supplies commonly disappeared from factory floors and reappeared on a sales table in a local marketplace. Workers exchanged more important items, such as generators, conveyer belts, and stamping machines, for certain items they desired, including spare parts for their cars, new clothing, television sets, or appliances. Because money was generally scarce in Russia, this system of barter grew in importance, even though it was illegal.

Whether stolen by the pocketful or by the truckload, valuable goods found their way to the vast underground market that supplied Russian consumers outside the legal distribution channels. Author Yuri Tarnopolsky, in his book *Memoirs of 1984*, describes the situation as follows:

> Over several decades . . . an amazing set of double standards regarding property

Workplaces such as this one had tight security checks at their entrances in an effort to curtail theft.

has developed. Although it was "our" government, its property was "theirs." Stealing from other people was a sin, but stealing from the government was not.

Paint, meat, timber, nails, paper, thread, drugs, scissors, eggs, alcohol, glass—all that was being stolen, often by those who were supposed to guard it.

The thieves thought they were justified because even more grain, cement, steel, vegetables, and valuable equipment perished beneath the snow and under the rain. It was devoured by rust, frost, mildew, carelessness, irresponsibility, and the lack of a real owner. Meanwhile, the stores were empty.[30]

In an attempt to stop these thefts and diversions, most workplaces in Communist Russia had very tight security checks at their entrances. Guards would stop all outsiders from entering the place of business unless they had some good reason for being there. Despite these efforts, economic crime worsened as the Soviet system failed to deliver consumer goods or the "workers' paradise." Bribery of officials, extortion, and the embezzlement of money from offices and factories became common. One of the most prominent economic crimes in Communist Russia was "speculation," or buying and selling goods privately for profit. Individuals accused of speculation were hauled into court and put through a public trial. If found guilty, they could be punished by up to five years in jail.

Living with the Black Market

The system of *blat*, or mutual aid, operated as energetically in the workplace as it did in the private lives of Russian workers. Favors were exchanged between workers and among management. To arrange an extended vacation, for example, a worker might arrange for fresh vegetables from his private garden to be delivered to the official responsible for making up a work schedule. Managers, in turn, often had to rely on bribes to procure their raw materials and supplies, or to arrange repair of their machinery.

Private and informal dealing was often the only way to keep a workplace running and productive. One farm manager explained how the system worked:

> We took a tractor engine to be repaired. When I sent a mechanic to collect it, he came back without it. When I asked him the problem, he said: "In return for the engine they want a sheep." So we had to slaughter one and send him back with it. In the old days they would fix things for a bottle of brandy. Now they want a sheep. What it will be next I don't know."[31]

The basic socialist theory, that central planning would bring about the most efficient method of work as well as economic justice for workers, did not materialize in Communist Russia. Instead, the system devised by Marx and Lenin resulted in a waste of resources and corruption throughout every Russian company and organization, as well as exploitation of a new sort by the bosses and by the state.

Keeping Track of Workers

Connections and influence played a central role in the careers of Russia's managers. In

---

Working for Little

The ordinary Russian worker had little incentive to do a good job. According to socialist theory, salaries should cover only basic, everyday expenses; as a result, beating a production goal brought a bonus but rarely a raise. The state set low prices for basic expenses—including rent, transportation, food, and fuel—and since most goods were scarce, there were few "nonessential" items to spend one's money on anyway. The Soviet economy provided few of the luxuries of life, such as automobiles, that ordinary people saw as worth working for. As a result of these practices, large savings accounts were common among workers in Communist Russia.

Most workers also could not look forward to promotion. There was little chance for a worker to rise within a company to the ranks of management. Promotion came only with personal connections to managers or to government bureaucrats in charge of each industry. On the other hand, there was also little fear of losing one's job for misconduct or low production. A job was guaranteed to everyone, and the constant demand for higher production created a scarcity of labor throughout the country. Such scarcity was frustrating to objective observers, who were aware of overstaffing in many enterprises but who were prevented, by five-year plans and other artifacts of central planning, from moving workers superfluous in one business to offices or factories that really needed them.

the Communist system, the bosses obtained their jobs through government appointments, which were rewarded to political allies or to loyal Communist Party members. In turn, the bosses held authority over the distribution of employees' salaries, work schedules, rewards and punishments, vacation time, and other privileges.

To keep track of the workers, many bosses used a system of paid informants. The informants reported acts of disloyalty, subversive conversations, laziness, drunkenness, arguments, and sabotage. The citizens of Communist Russia, in their work as well as in their private lives, were expected to police each other and watch out for any transgressions.

To punish the disobedient, the bosses might hold meetings on a certain day of the week, which came to be known as "Clean Tuesday" or "Clean Wednesday." Here the workers could publicly denounce others, who were then expected to confess to their incompetence or their lack of loyalty or enthusiasm. At these meetings, workers also might discuss their performance, production quotas and plans, and minor offenses committed by fellow workers. These sessions often extended into the workers' private lives; the workers often had to respond to charges of drunkenness, adultery, or defiance of authority in one form or another.

The entire work history of each individual was recorded in a *kharakteristika*, or labor performance book. Workers had to keep these books in a safe place and show them to all prospective employers. The books listed all hirings, firings, promotions, and demotions— no matter what their cause. The labor books reminded Russian workers that their limited freedoms depended greatly on their perceived loyalty. Those who reached the society's elite, who had better apartments, the right to shop in well-stocked stores, the right

to travel abroad, and the like, did not want to lose these rights through acts of disloyalty to the system or to their employers. Once this happened, regaining their former status was nearly impossible.

Labor Unions

Workers in Communist Russia were not required to join labor unions, but such membership—like membership in the Communist Party—made it easier for them to advance in their careers. Russian unions were not organized by company or by factory. Instead, each union included all of the workers in a certain industry, and all the workers in a single place of work belonged to the same national union.

Russian labor unions were supposed to share responsibility with management in setting quotas, wages, working conditions, schedules, and so on. The labor union was also a form of recreational club, which arranged vacations and sporting activities for its members. As representatives of the workers, they were—in theory—supposed to act and argue for the workers' benefit. In fact, trade unions in Communist Russia were simply another form of management serving to supervise and discipline workers.

The heads of each union carried out these functions through a weekly meeting, at which they criticized or praised individual workers and explained the policies of management. Unions could appeal individual cases of workers getting fired or try to enforce safety conditions through the court system. But strikes, work slowdowns, or other forms of labor activism were illegal and almost never took place in Communist Russia.

Under such conditions, managers and labor bosses understood that they must provide some kind of benefit to their workers. The benefit came in the form of recreation, sport, limited travel, and frequent reminders—in the press and in state-approved books and works of art—that the Russian worker enjoyed a lifestyle that the people of tsarist times could not have imagined.

Recreation on the Job

Russians did not spend their entire workday in work. Communist philosophy held that the health and happiness of the workers should be important goals of any enterprise. Every

Gigantism

As a sign of their nation's progress, the leaders of Communist Russia favored large industrial projects: huge dams, immense steel and concrete factories, canals and railroads that crossed hundreds of miles of wasteland. One of the most ambitious projects under Communist rule was a plan to reverse the flow of several major Siberian rivers in order to irrigate arid land to the south, a project that ultimately failed.

This industrial "gigantism" extended to the official names of industrial and political organizations. The names could be so long and convoluted that, instead of explaining the function of an organization, they completely obscured it. The Guinness Book of World Records 1998 cites one Communist-era acronym as the world's longest: NIIOMT-PLABOPARMBETZHELBETRABSBOM ONIMONKONOTDTEKHSTROMONT, which stood for Laboratory for Shuttering Reinforcement, Concrete, and Ferroconcrete Operations for Composite-Monolithic and Monolithic Constructions of the Department of the Technology of Building-Assembly Operations of the Scientific Research Institute of the Organization for Building Mechanization and Technical Aid of the Academy of Building and Architecture of the USSR.

Russians labor on a canal in Siberia.

Measuring the Worker

In Communist Russia, the state's propaganda extolled the exploits of workers who met and exceeded production quotas. Within the factory, however, the worker was regarded only as a unit that contributed toward fulfilling the plan. Writer David Satter in *Age of Delirium*, describes the result of rigid adherence to the plan.

"The focus shifts from the character of the article being manufactured to quantities—units, tons, kilometers—the only means through which plan fulfillment can be assessed. In the process, workers are turned into robots. If gross output is calculated in rubles, they [managers] add useless, expensive details; if it is calculated in weight, they use the heaviest materials; if it is measured in kilometer-hours, they send transports back and forth between distant cities."

factory in Russia held a daily break for exercise. Machines were left silent as the workers left the factory floor for an exercise yard or a large indoor gymnasium. When production demands were high, workers might remain near their assigned places doing calisthenics for a few minutes before resuming work.

Some factories also had relaxation rooms, which were areas set aside for workers to relax and get rid of stress. Workers, with the permission of their supervisors, could use the relaxation rooms for a certain amount of time each day or each week. Some of the rooms had comfortable furniture, books and magazines to read, and soft music to listen to. But others had only hard chairs and tables. The factory's managers decided how to furnish such rooms or whether to provide them at all.

Soviet factories also sponsored their own organized athletic clubs and sports teams. Workers favored ice hockey, basketball, and especially soccer, and many of these clubs carried out intense and long-lasting rivalries with other cities and companies. Factories also sponsored vacation trips to the seacoast and expeditions into the mountains, as well as travel to foreign destinations for workers who had permission to leave the country. For many workers dedicated by the state to a collective effort, these vacations away from a collective society became the highest goal, to be sought and worked for ahead of all other benefits.

Chapter 5

Sports and Leisure Time

Russian Communist society placed a heavy emphasis on physical conditioning and participation in sports. Every large city had its Palace of Sports, where citizens holding passes could use basketball courts, indoor tracks, and swimming pools. Soccer fields dotted the outskirts of towns large and small, and in most cities a stadium was available for the use of local teams.

Sports were a way of enforcing a collective spirit among citizens, and also of encouraging loyalty to party organizations. In many ways, sports teams imitated military units. In both organizations, leaders emphasized discipline and cooperation as the most important characteristics of the good performer. All Russian athletes saw themselves as part of a team first and as individuals second.

There were many state organizations for aspiring young athletes. The most important of them was the GTO, whose Russian initials stood for "Ready for Work and Defense." The GTO had different levels for varying age groups, starting at the age of ten. The GTO ranked its members in each individual sport. Its purpose was to prepare the most talented young athletes for national or Olympic teams.

One of the highest public honors for a Russian citizen was the GTO badge. To win the badge, aspirants had to pass a series of physical challenges, running, swimming, weapons training, and first aid. The GTO program was meant to promote fitness as well as military preparedness on the part of the public.

Playing for the Company Team

Sports and physical conditioning were not considered part-time or leisure-time activities in Communist Russia. Sports collectives organized in offices, schools, and factories. The workers in most large factories could join company sports teams or make use of gymnasiums and exercise facilities on the factory grounds. One of the nation's largest plants, the Moskvich car factory in Moscow, boasted a huge sports complex with swimming pools, soccer fields, tennis and basketball courts, and a velodrome, or bicycle racing track.

Many of Russia's star Olympic athletes began their athletic careers on such company teams. Since there were no professional athletes in Russia, even the best swimmers, runners, and wrestlers held regular jobs. But the country's best athletes enjoyed easy work assignments, and athletes good enough to make Olympic and national amateur teams enjoyed a high status in Russian society. They also were awarded favors reserved for privileged citizens and state officials, such as regular pensions and foreign travel.

Another kind of athlete honored by the people of Communist Russia was the skilled chess player. Nearly everyone in Russia knew the game of chess and took great pride in the achievements of Russian champions such as Boris Spassky, who proved too much for most of his opponents from the West. Russians looking for a game of chess or checkers needed only to walk down to a local park, where a series of games were likely to be under way, observed by crowds of spectators.

After Work

In their homes, Russians favored listening to the radio or watching television, if they owned a set. But perhaps the favorite leisure-time activity among the people of Communist Russia was reading, a pastime instilled in students from a young age. Russians honored their poets and writers above all creative artists, and many Russians could quote long passages from the works of great nineteenth-century novelists such as Tolstoy, Turgenev, and Dostoyevsky. But in their day-to-day lives, Russians also had to be careful about which writers they mentioned and praised. Admiring the works of authors not favored by the state could bring a warning from colleagues or party officials.

There were two basic kinds of books, plays, stories, and articles in Communist Russia: official and unofficial. Authors who worked without the approval of government committees could only print and distribute their works secretly, "unofficially." Most such underground artists worked at ordinary jobs, and rather than earning money and fame from writing, they risked arrest and exile for disloyalty to the regime. After World War II, the works of unofficial writers gained a wider audience throughout Russia through samizdat publishing, in which handwritten or photocopied versions of their works passed from one clandestine reader to the next.

To earn any kind of living by their writing, "official" authors in Communist Russia had to work under the very close supervision of the state. They were collected into a union, the Union of Soviet Writers, which examined their works for any signs of "decadence," or attitudes opposing socialism and favoring the societies and political systems of Western Europe or the United States. The principal function of the writer was to praise the system,

Boris Spassky (right) was a champion chess player and a national hero.

Going to the Movies

Movies were a passion for many Russians and going to see Western movies was the greatest privilege of all. Most films from Europe and the United States, however, were not allowed into the country. Those that did arrive were copied and stored in a large and secure vault. A special committee, the State Committee of Cinematography, controlled the release of these films to cinemas, where tickets were given out to the social and government elite. David K. Shipler describes the system in his book *Russia: Broken Idols, Solemn Dreams*:

"The copies, usually in black and white or poor-quality color and dubbed into Russian by a flatly read translation in one voice, are stored in a vast underground archive at the northern edge of Moscow, from which they can be lent to the closed clubs or the dachas of the powerful, whose country homes are often equipped with projectors.

In the evenings, at seven-thirty or eight, a highly restricted audience is admitted to a theater on the fourth floor of the state committee's office building at 7 Maly Gnezdnikovsky Lane to see first-run American and Western European films whose violence, explicit sex, and social themes are deemed inappropriate for viewing by ordinary, unprivileged Russians. Those inside the hall are carefully selected, holding passes supposedly given because of their professional interest. But just as Stalin loved American westerns, the Soviet elite today covets its access to the taboos from the outside world; touching some facet of the West is a mark of status and a source of craving and thus a valuable coin of affluence, spent carefully."

urge its members to attain greater productivity, and to strengthen their dedication to achieving the utopian Communist future.

The Official News

The government jealously guarded information as well as entertainment, and kept control of all electronic media as well as the written word. The nightly television news program, known as Vremya, formed the principal outlet for news about the state's leaders and their policies. Television news anchors, as well as newspaper reporters, gave the news of the day in sterile, nearly meaningless bureaucratic phrases that described and explained very little. To ordinary Russians, who knew that all information in their country was tightly controlled, watching and reading the news became a kind of game or puzzle in which the state's policies could only be guessed at through the images or stories that appeared in print or on the TV screen. The position of an important official on a parade-reviewing stand in a photograph, for example, might indicate his rise or fall in the ranks of the government. The space given in a newspaper to a certain speech on government policy, which might seem to say very little, showed the actual importance that Russian leaders attached to it.

Television programs emphasized the achievements of the nation's industry, innovations in Russian science, and the achievements of the past, especially the heroic performance of Russian armies during World War II. Russian Olympic athletes and athletic

Pravda was the official newspaper of Communist Russia.

teams also were covered; television programs featured ice hockey, soccer, and basketball games, as well as important chess matches.

On the Big Screen

Russian citizens also enjoyed an evening at the cinema, although most towns had only one cinema open and a very limited menu of features to show. The state banned most foreign movies but permitted films imported from other Communist nations such as the People's Republic of China and Central European Communist countries. All films made in Russia had to follow a strict format. The hero had to exemplify Communist ideals, and the conclusion of the film had to glorify the Communist state and its achievements. Government censors passed or rejected movie scripts according to the rules laid down by the government.

The tight restrictions on movie scripts and subject matter, according to Harrison Salisbury, paralyzed the Russian film industry:

It took two years to bring out a picture which easily could be filmed in two months. And the public stayed away in droves. Only occasionally when a semimusical like *Kuban Cossack* was sneaked through the projection room did the thousands of film houses in Russia have anything that would draw. And each of those houses had a "profit plan" to fulfill. It drove the managers crazy. . . .

Only one thing drew the public. In 1945, the Red Army had captured a library of one or two hundred old American pictures in Berlin. . . . Of all the American pictures the one which was the record hit . . . was Johnny Weismuller in *Tarzan*. In the Red Army's captured film bag there were four old Weismuller Tarzans. They were fed out, one at a time, into the Soviet houses over a two-year period. People lined up for blocks to get in. Youngsters saw them again and again. Children often sat through a whole day's showing in a movie house.[32]

The Soviet government also set up a large production company, known as Mosfilm, to produce movies. Mosfilm had its own writers, film editors, directors, actors, and producers. The company also controlled a network of theaters that showed only Mosfilm productions. Actors working for Mosfilm were assigned their roles by the heads of the studio and had little control over these decisions.

When not acting in a film, they worked at a Moscow studio theater, where they honed their talents in front of a live audience. Mosfilm actors also provided voices for foreign films dubbed into Russian.

Dining Out

An evening out for a Russian often meant going to a restaurant, a big social occasion in which friends and family formed a large group and tried to enjoy themselves to the fullest. Restaurants, however, were not very common, and those that operated required reservations well in advance for all their customers. Typically, Russian restaurants opened at 6:00 P.M.; closing time was 11:00 P.M., unless the management

made an exception for a large group or for those accompanying a high-ranking official or local party boss.

Many Russian restaurants operated cafeteria style, with customers sidling up to a long serving table, where workers delivered food, drink, and dessert. The cafeteria restaurant did not always emphasize good service on the part of its employees:

Here the customer is not always right. He asks, he is humble, he tries to obtain service, without being at all sure of success. The roubles in his pocket do not confer any superiority on him. The master in this situation is the woman in the white blouse on the other side of the counter. She serves you with majestic

Tarzan movies became a big screen sensation in Communist Russia at the end of World War II.

slowness, showing by her every gesture and word that she is not absolutely sure of your right to service, that she is perhaps being a little too kind to you, that after all nothing forces her to sell you that crab paste or that herring, that loaf of bread or that tin of cocoa.[33]

At the Circus

In their leisure time, Russians also enjoyed circus performances. Traveling circuses made their rounds through the vast country, stopping on the outskirts of towns and cities to set up their tents and provide spectators with the acts of clowns, weightlifters, trapeze artists, trained animals, gymnasts, and other performers.

The country's largest circus, the Moscow State Circus, traveled all over the world. Many of the performers in the Moscow State Circus spent years training in a specialized institute for circus performers. Many of them also worked their way up from smaller local circuses or worked as gymnasts or stage actors.

To be hired by the Moscow Circus was to reach the top of one's profession. At the same time, the performers worked as hard as anyone in the country. The state could not put a production quota on the skill of an acrobat or the humor of a clown, but audiences did rate their performances, as audiences did everywhere else in the world, by their attention, applause, and enthusiasm. Retired or declining performers suffered exile to local circuses or to less glamorous jobs as trainers and assistants.

In exchange for their hard work, the performers of Russian circuses enjoyed freedoms denied to other people working in the arts. Clowns, for example, could devise their own acts, which often had very little to do with outrageous costumes, bulbous red noses, or other hallmarks of traditional circus comedy. Some of these acts came close to outright criticism of the system under which the people lived. Joan Hasler, in her book *The Making of Russia*, describes a clown's deadly criticism, under the veil of humor, of the travails of Communist bureaucracy:

> A timid citizen comes to apply for a post and is kept hanging about for no reason except that the bureaucrat wants to have several more swigs in secret at his bottle of vodka. When he condescends to see

the common little man at last he fires questions at him like bullets from a machine gun. Has he got his card of identification, photograph of himself, his wife, his children, parents, and parents-in-law, all their marriage and birth certificates, references from previous places of employment, legal certificates of discharge, school certificates, certificate of national service, and so on? At each request the little man slapped the relevant documents on the desk while the bureaucrat got obviously more and more perturbed that he might in the end have no excuse for turning down the applicant. The final despairing question was, "Have you got your mother-in-law's fingerprints?" When these too were triumphantly produced [the official] pulled out a pistol from his desk and shot himself. [34]

Recreation and Vacations

One of the most common leisure-time outings for Russian citizens was to spend the day in a city park. The largest parks offered hiking paths, carnival rides, theaters, cinemas, and restaurants. During the summer, visitors rowed canoes on lakes and ponds; during the long, cold winters, ice skaters used the many large stretches of frozen water. Some parks offered small oval tracks that catered to an age-old enthusiasm of the Russian people: watching and betting on horse races.

The Russian is a gambler—gambler enough for young officers to have invented, in times gone by, that fatal pastime called Russian roulette. . . . It is also the country of the Cossacks and the people love horses. These two factors make racing and betting on races inevitable. In a decision of 27 December 1948 the Central Committee of the Communist Party laid down detailed regulations governing all aspects of equestrian sport. [35]

According to these regulations, Russian gamblers could bet on horses only to win and not, as elsewhere in the world, to finish second or third. (This method cut an individual's chances of winning any money on a single race considerably.) The state collected all bets, handed out the winnings, and kept the rest to maintain its own breeding farms. Jockeys in Russia collected fixed salaries but also won bonuses for their victories and for good results turned in by the training facilities where they worked.

Horse racing took place in all seasons and at all times of the year. There was no break for the harsh, long months of winter. In fact, Russians have long felt a strong attachment to the winter season. On a day off in winter, a Russian family might venture out into the countryside for cross-country skiing through the immense pine or birch forests that cover the northern half of their country. Russians also enjoyed visiting natural mineral springs year-round. Many believed that bathing in thermal springs improved their health and offered them a chance to escape cancer, heart disease, and other life-threatening illnesses.

On their summer vacation, Russians sought the warmth and leisurely atmosphere of the seaside. But for the vast majority, there was only one warm seacoast to visit: the Black Sea, which lay within the Ukrainian Soviet Socialist Republic (now Ukraine). Every summer, great crowds of vacationing Russians traveled south to gather in Black Sea resorts, lay in the sun, cavort on the beach, and wade close to the shore.

Russians celebrated their Communist philosophies and achievements on May 1, also called May Day.

Communist Holidays

More important, officially, than any vacation or family outing were Russia's national holidays. The most important of these marked the Bolshevik revolution on November 7. All over Russia, the local party committees oversaw the decoration of their main squares with signs, banners, red flags, and portraits of Lenin and other Communist heroes. A military parade wound through the central streets of each city, followed by a procession of civilian leaders and officials. The local Young Pioneers and Komsomol members took their place in the procession, followed by designated heroes of local factories and collective farms.

Another occasion for national celebration fell on May 1, or May Day. On May Day, socialist and Communist parties all over the world celebrated their philosophy and their achievements. Russian citizens took part in festive parades, carrying banners and listening to patriotic music. On this day, more than any other, Russian citizens felt like a part of an international community. Yet in the capital, Moscow, it was not always possible for ordinary citizens to join in the festivities, as journalist David K. Shipler explains:

> The parades . . . are pageants of military might and worker solidarity, done in the name of the common man, but not open to him. Admission is by ticket only, a ticket carefully provided to those deemed worthy. The streets in central Moscow are closed to unauthorized vehicles and pedestrians; from my apartment just over a quarter of a mile away, I had to pass thirteen checkpoints to the November 7 parade—five in my car, with the proper document, then eight more on foot.[36]

These state-sanctioned holidays offered Russians a chance to take time off, join in and observe public ceremonies, and relax from the pressures of work and school. Yet for many people, unofficial holidays and ceremonies marked the most important days of the year. These holidays were celebrated quietly, sometimes in secret, for they were inspired by a nearly illegal aspect of daily life: religion.

6 Religion

In Communist Russia, Marxism-Leninism was regarded as the basis for the perfect society, the chart that would guide the workers to a future utopia. According to this philosophy, political leaders, wise in the proper workings of the socialist state, would quickly replace religious leaders, whose outmoded beliefs had no place in a scientifically managed nation. Religion was considered useless superstition, whereas communism was considered a science, a completely objective way of thinking and acting. In this system, each individual took responsibility for contributing to the good of all, and only the party could judge their success or failure in this regard. There was no place in Communist society for Christian doctrines that promised salvation and an afterlife in paradise for the virtuous individual, as measured by the tenets of the Bible. Under communism, the Russian Orthodox Church, the traditional church of the Russian people for nearly a thousand years, was supposed to disappear.

Communism and the Church

After the revolution of 1917, the Bolshevik government began a campaign of propaganda and legal action against the Orthodox Eastern Church (comprising Christian denominations in Russia and other nations that had split from the Roman Catholic pope in the eleventh century). Party officials in each town and village were given the authority to close any churches they wished, even though these churches, large and small, had served even the smallest and most isolated Russian village as both a spiritual retreat and a community center. The state imprisoned or executed Orthodox priests and closed their seminaries and other places of learning. Soldiers and

St. Basil's cathedral is a monument to Russian Orthodox Christianity.

state police removed religious icons (religious images of Jesus or the saints that were painted on small wood panels). New saints, canonized by the Bolshevik revolution, appeared in public and private places:

Portraits of Lenin in the "red corner" of factories, stores, theaters, schools, public buildings and kolkhoz offices have replaced the icons of Christ and the Virgin in the "icon corner" of tsarist days. Pictures of the Soviet leaders, the members of the Politburo are today deployed in a prescribed order of importance on either side of a portrait of Lenin. They have replaced the old iconostasis, the screen of Russian Orthodox churches, in which saints were arranged in a fixed order to

The Apotheosis of Lenin

The transformation of communism into the "religion" of Russia was symbolized by the elaborate funeral held for Lenin, the founder of the state. After the ceremonies, the body of Lenin was embalmed and placed in a shrine that stood on one side of Red Square, the huge central square of Moscow. During parades and state ceremonies, the leaders of the country appeared on the rostrum atop the tomb. Below them lay the dead Lenin, reposing in a casket made of strong, bulletproof glass, an object of wonderment to the crowds of citizens and tourists that formed long lines outside the mausoleum. The visit to Lenin's tomb became a sort of religious pilgrimage for Communist citizens, one that millions of visitors from small towns and villages made whenever they visited the capital.

the left and right of Christ enthroned. Even the principle of the icon procession has been retained in May Day and Revolution Day parades through Red Square, where huge portraits of the leaders and Lenin are held aloft by the crowd.[37]

Churches that were not torn down became social centers, meeting halls, warehouses, local museums, or sports centers. The condition of surviving churches gradually deteriorated. Many grew unsafe and had to be boarded up or demolished. In this way, Russia lost many of its most important historical monuments.

All over the country, Russians seeking to attend religious services found they had no place to congregate. Moreover, they now had to fear punishment for holding to their beliefs. The Communist Party denied party membership, and all the privileges such membership carried, to any individual who professed Christianity or who still belonged to the Orthodox church as a priest or lay leader.

Such discrimination also extended to Jewish Russians, who were prohibited from teaching or publishing in Hebrew and who saw their synagogues closed or destroyed. The state considered Jewishness a nationality as well as a religion, and it marked internal passports and legal documents accordingly. After the founding of Israel in 1948, many Russian Jews applied to leave Russia and to emigrate to Israel (those whom the state rejected were known as "refuseniks"). Those who remained in Russia were subject to the same antireligious practices directed against Christians. The American Jewish writer Chaim Potok, in his book *The Gates of November*, describes one such event:

An antireligion campaign began to sweep through much of the country. . . . It was

A Jewish man reads a Yiddish newspaper. Jews were prohibited from teaching or publishing in Hebrew.

directed against not only Judaism but all faiths. About fifty synagogues—"nests of speculators," rose the cry from the local press—and thousands of churches were shut down. The last synagogue in the city of Minsk had its roof removed during a service and was turned into a club. Baking the traditional Passover flatbread, matzah, was forbidden. And a campaign against economic crimes netted an astonishing number of Jews, whose names were prominently announced in the press.[38]

Surviving Under Communism

Churches that did remain open were subject to heavy taxation. At the end of each year, those that had any money saved in bank accounts had to turn over all of their money to the state. The church could not proselytize or send missionaries abroad. Its leaders could not participate in government or in local community affairs. Propaganda in official books and newspapers painted the church as a backward and useless relic of the past, one best abandoned by true believers in the socialist future.

Russian Orthodoxy survived this treatment. Party officials allowed some Orthodox churches to carry on services and stay open to visitors and worshipers. Moreover, a majority of Russian Christians, especially those who had reached adulthood before the revolution of 1917, did not abandon their beliefs. In many places, the home became the only place where the members of a family could practice traditional forms of piety. For this reason, Russians sometimes built small shrines in a corner of their living rooms or on the top of a cabinet. Many Russian families also decorated their homes with crucifixes and with icons, an important form of Russian religious art for centuries. Many Russians also continued observing the rites of the most important Orthodox holidays: Easter and Christmas.

Russian believers observed Christmas with a fast that began forty days before the holiday, which in the Orthodox calendar falls on January 6. During the fast, faithful Christians did

The Orthodox Service

The traditional Russian Orthodox service was carried on in Slavonic, an old form of the Russian language. The deacon of the church pronounced a call, and the gathered priests responded, while worshipers stood in the center of the church, making the sign of the cross, and quietly repeating the familiar words of the liturgy. Along the walls were rows of icons and other images that told the story of Jesus and the apostles.

The service carried an especially profound meaning during the holiday seasons of Easter and Christmas, as writer Michael Binyon explains.

"To be in a working Russian church immediately gives you a sense of eternal Russia, and makes it clear why beauty and ritual, the sense of history and continuity hold such appeal for young people seeking spiritual truths beyond the drabness and cynicism of modern life. I vividly remember the midnight service at Suzdal on Christmas Eve: the moon glittering on the fresh snow, the decorated wooden houses looking warm and bright in the freezing night, worshippers streaming out of the white-washed church as the bells rang out the Christmas message. . . .

The congregation of about 200 were packed in suffocating closeness, mainly old women, in black shawls and headscarves muffling wrinkled, harsh faces that showed a lifetime of struggle and suffering. They chanted the responses in quavering voices, shuffling about in their heavy felt boots and crossing themselves frequently before the many icons with their rows of burning candles."

not eat eggs or meat. Russian families did not exchange gifts, but they did recognize the kindly figure of Grandfather Frost, *Dyet oroz*, a bearded old gentleman who rides a troika pulled by horses and who carries his presents through the front door. (In some locales, Grandfather Frost was accompanied by *Snyegorouchka*, the Snow Maiden.)

On Christmas Eve, young girls went door-to-door to sing carols; boys did the same on the following morning. If Orthodox priests were still living in the community, the members of their congregations arrived at their front door to offer a traditional Christmas meal of rice, nuts, wheat, and mead, a sweet wine made from honey.

The Easter holiday, like Christmas in the West, made up a distinct period of the Russian calendar that lasted several weeks. In the days before Easter, Russian families dressed in their finest clothes and paid visits to the graves of their deceased relatives. They spruced up the graves and left small offerings of flowers, food, and sometimes small glasses of vodka. Despite their state ownership, local bakeries prepared Easter cakes known as *kulich*. These cakes were eaten with a butter and raisin pudding known as *paskha*. Painting and decorating Easter eggs formed another central activity of the Easter holiday.

One of the most familiar aspects of Easter in Russia was the sound of bells ringing out from the local church or cathedral at midnight on Easter Saturday. In Moscow, the ringing of the bells began in the heart of the city in the old fortress of the Kremlin:

During the night of Easter Saturday the great bell of the [Cathedral of the] Assumption used to peal out its powerful voice of bronze, a signal to all the bells of Moscow to start ringing for midnight mass, the zaoutrina of the Russians; when this is over, the faithful exchange a triple kiss of peace, proclaiming that Christ has risen from the dead.[39]

Rival Ceremonies

Ordinary Russians observed religious traditions and holidays without risking jail or punishment. But they did often experience public tauntings, especially from Communist Party leaders, for their faith. Especially committed believers might also see their professional careers suffer by the lack of a promotion or the withholding of privileges. Their children might draw the scorn of classmates or the neglect of their teachers. Membership in the Young Pioneers and Komsomol was usually denied to young Orthodox believers.

The leaders of Communist Russia believed that, with the advancement of communism, religious belief, like the state, would gradually wither away. To hurry this process along, the state came up with secular substitutes for the traditional church ceremonies and holidays. One of these was "Naming Day." On this day, parents brought their newborns and infants into Communist society with a short legal ceremony at a town hall or civic center. The presiding officials awarded a certificate to the family and recognized the appointment of two friends as guardians. The state intended Naming Day to replace the Christian practice of baptism, at which Russian parents named their infants and selected each child's godfather and godmother.

Traditionally, Russian Orthodoxy also celebrated a new marriage. Although the Communist state did not recognize church or synagogue weddings, it participated in these events by demanding that certain documents be filled out and certain procedures followed.

The Doctors' Plot

Toward the end of his life, Joseph Stalin's fears and suspicions grew more intense. Certain that his enemies, as well as his friends, were out to get him, and especially suspicious of Jews, Stalin contrived the "Doctors' Plot" in late 1952 to solve both problems. Nine high-ranking doctors who worked in the Kremlin were accused of poisoning or otherwise killing Communist officials. Seven of the suspects were Jewish. All were interrogated and tortured. Stalin may have ultimately planned a public hanging in Red Square for the accused.

Many Jewish doctors, religious leaders, and scientists were rounded up by the secret police. Prompted by sensational newspaper stories, ordinary Russians began to fear that Jews were contaminating their water, their food, and their prescription drugs. The government persuaded several Jewish leaders to sign a petition asking for the removal of the Jews to the Russian Far East. Stalin wanted to be seen as rescuing the Jews by allowing them to move as far as possible from western Russia, where most of them had their homes and made their livelihoods.

Stalin's death on March 5, 1953, ended the outcry. The "Doctors' Plot" turned out to be a figment of the diseased mind of a dying dictator.

The End of Icons

Among the Orthodox believers of Russia, the painted icon provided a simple and powerful representation of the founders of their church and the doctrines of their faith. Under the Communist system, however, icons suffered a harsh punishment at the hands of those who saw them as potent antistate propaganda. In *Imperium*, a description of his journey through the remote regions of the Soviet Union, writer Ryszard Kapuscinski details the icons' destruction.

"That same wild and primal, and later premeditated and methodical, barbarism that ruined and demolished the churches also destroyed the icon.

How many icons fell victim to it?

From October 1917 until [the 1990s], twenty, thirty, million icons were destroyed in Russia!

This figure is cited by the Russian art historian A. Kuzniecov in the monthly *Moskva* (January 1990). Kuzniecov lists the destructive uses icons were put to:

In the army—for target practice.

In the mines—as pavement for tunnels flooded with water.

In the market place—as raw material for building potato crates.

In kitchens—as boards for chopping meat and vegetables.

In apartments—as fuel for stoves in winter."

The author adds that massive piles of icons were also simply set afire or driven out to country and city garbage dumps.

(Many wedding couples attended two separate ceremonies, one secular and official and the other religious. This is still the practice in much of Western, capitalist Europe.) To get married in Communist Russia, one had to go through the proper bureaucratic procedure:

> When the time comes for a citizen to get married, he is once again dependent on documents. After a couple announce their intention to wed, the first step is to fill out a questionnaire to qualify for a marriage license. When their documents are accepted, a stamp is put in the couple's passports that gives them the right to purchase rugs, shoes, and other clothing in a special wedding store. It also allows them to reserve a limousine.[40]

Many cities and small towns operated a public Palace of Weddings where a series of very brief wedding ceremonies took place under the direction of a local party official. For each couple, the presiding official delivered a short address and a pronouncement that they are now man and wife. One such ceremony was witnessed and described by Andrew Wachtel and Eugene Zykov in their photo essay *At the Dawn of Glasnost*:

> We watch a nervous bride and groom sign the marriage register and, with fumbling hands, put rings on each other's fingers. A tape of the Kremlin chimes fills the air with plangent tones as the bride and groom kiss. The orchestra strikes up a popular tune, "We Wish You A Happy Married Life." The bride and groom accept the congratulations of well-wishers as they are all hustled out of the ceremonial chamber through a side door. Now they will drive all around Moscow along an official "wedding route," stopping to place flowers on the

Many cities operated a public Palace of Weddings directed by a public official where couples could wed instead of having a traditional religious ceremony.

grave of the unknown soldier and pausing at the Lenin Hills for a panoramic view of the city.[41]

Despite such blatant attempts to replace one set of cultural traditions with another, Russia's Communist government did not succeed in completely suppressing the religious rites of baptisms, marriages, and funerals. Indeed, these ceremonies played an important role in supporting the struggling church, whose authorities arranged them in exchange for small fees donated by the participants and offerings from onlookers and guests.

In the case of a death, the deceased's passport had to be turned over to the authorities. Then, and only then, could a death certificate be issued, which was in turn required to purchase a coffin from the state funeral store. All places in a cemetery had to be approved and assigned by the appropriate local official. Gravestones and other markers had to follow certain height and size restrictions.

Because the doctrines and liturgy of the church remained outside of state control, religious institutions were held suspect, outside of acceptable Communist society. Nevertheless, the Orthodox Church remained an essential part of Russian culture for the Russian people. Older people, in particular, continued attending services where and when they could, displaying icons in their home and observing the rites of Christmas and Easter.

Fashionable Religion

For many Russians struggling to cope with a difficult life and a bewildering political system, Christianity served as a link to a simpler past. Although the state's official history books painted Orthodox history and practices as a superstitious, backward, ignorant, and forgettable part of their culture, it gradually became fashionable among the Russians to display the trappings of religion, such as icons nailed to the walls of the home and religious jewelry worn on the body. By the 1980s, young Russians were wearing crucifixes as well as religious T-shirts with images of Jesus or the Virgin Mary. Many Russian writers and artists infused their works with religious mysticism and Orthodox symbols. The Russians turned to the church and to church services as a form of protest against the ideological proselytizing of the state.

New sects of Christianity also gained strength, even under official state disapproval and repression of religion. The most significant of these was Baptism, a Protestant sect that banned the use of alcohol (a solution to a very common ill among all classes of Russians). Baptists formed tightly knit communities in many Russian cities and towns. Like all church organizations, Baptists were required to register with the state; otherwise, the organization was considered illegal. Those who didn't register had to meet in secret. But the Russian Baptists were aggressive recruiters who enjoyed the attraction of any other underground movement among the Russians, who often took the opportunity to join such a sect just for the sake of making a small gesture of defiance toward the rules and regulations that enveloped their daily lives.

Art, Literature, and Music

Russians had always admired the works of their creative artists and considered many of their poems, novels, and musical works important national achievements. In addition, the average Russian citizen took great pride in the collection of European masterworks in the Hermitage, a grand museum in the city of Leningrad. On the occasion of a visit to Leningrad, the Russian tourist always made sure to visit the Hermitage, just as visitors to Moscow always undertook a pilgrimage to Lenin's tomb in Red Square.

But artists working in modern Communist Russia had to be careful about their style and their subject matter. Under the Communist system, artists were expected to direct all forms of personal expression to a single end: glorifying the state, its workers, and their achievements. All artists were supposed to paint useful and realistic pictures, with their subject matter limited to industry, agriculture, and other facets of economic and working life. As a result, tractors, machinery, and enthusiastic laborers took a prominent place in approved Communist art, which embodied a style known both inside and outside of Russia as socialist realism.

Communist authorities demanded realism above all, and considered painting in an abstract or impressionistic style a telling symptom of Western decadence. As a result, most Russian painters could not make a personal study of the important twentieth-century art movements such as cubism or pop art that swept

through Western Europe and the United States. At the time these movements were gaining their first audiences, most Russians were not permitted to travel outside the country, and books and articles on the subject were not published inside Russia. Artists were strongly discouraged by officials, and by criticism from their peers, from making personal experiments in form or choosing original subject matter. The

Communist authorities approved only one type of art, referred to as "socialist realism."

state viewed all such individual effort as an expression of opposition to the collective spirit on which the Communist system was based.

The official Artists Union laid down guidelines for art in Communist Russia. The Artists Union enforced the government's directives and held control over patronage—the commissioning of artistic works by the state. All working artists were supposed to belong to this organization, and membership was a privilege that could be withdrawn at any time. Russian artists who earned the union's disapproval could not display their works in galleries, and individuals were not supposed to buy their works. In effect, Russians who did not belong to the Artists Union could not legally make a living by selling their art.

The Writer's Life

Many Communist Russian officials and party members distrusted intellectuals and considered those who wrote, painted, or played music for a living as useless parasites. Books, articles, magazines, and newspapers all came under the censorship of government agencies, and outright dissent from party policies became a crime in the 1920s. Indeed, any line of argument considered threatening to the regime, such as mild praise of Western capitalism or a positive description of an Orthodox congregation, came under scrutiny and suspicion. State officials did not allow disagreement with official policies laid down by party leaders, and they acknowledged those not adhering to the party line only to rebuke them in newspapers or other media.

The party extended the doctrine of socialist realism to literary as well as visual works. Writer J. N. Westwood explains:

Boris Pasternak was awarded a Nobel prize for literature for his novel Doctor Zhivago.

At various times Socialist Realism involved a multitude of restrictive concepts. In effect it meant that all artistic work should serve and further the Party line. Thus the hero in fiction was not necessarily to be lifelike; rather he was to be portrayed as the ideal Soviet man whom the Party was creating. Typically an upright and handsome young man, educated in Soviet schools, whose father was a lumberjack and mother a tram-driver (or vice-versa), who never wore a tie in his life, who was or would become a Party member, outproduced his fellows, overcame enemies of the people and saboteurs, loved Stalin and the Party, and never asked the wrong questions. Thus began a dreary succession of literary heroes like the champion tractor driver, or the grower of extra-large turnips with his hand on the spade and his eyes on the milkmaid (but never vice-versa) or the producer of double-norm and extra-quality ball-bearings who falls for a progressive bus conductress or revolutionary chambermaid.[42]

The state owned all book publishing houses, newspapers, and journals. Those books that were not approved by the heads of the Union of Soviet Writers—who followed a strict set of guidelines on vocabulary, style, subject matter, and acceptable opinion—were not published. The state jealously guarded its right to extend all awards and recognition, and considered literary popularity a danger to its authority. Boris Pasternak's novel *Doctor Zhivago*, a description of the troubles suffered by Russians in the wake of the Bolshevik revolution, was harshly condemned by leading party officials as an anti-revolutionary tract. Yet the book was widely read by Russian citizens and found an international audience; soon after writing it, the author was recognized with the Nobel prize for literature. Communist officials considered the Nobel prize a subversive Western institution, and they persuaded Pasternak not to accept the honor.

Other Russian writers did not escape harsher justice. The poet Osip Mandelstam died of starvation while being transported to a prison camp in 1938. Alexander Solzhenitsyn, a Russian officer, was sent to prison for telling a joke about Joseph Stalin in a private letter. After serving a long term in a gulag (labor camp) in Siberia, Solzhenitsyn wrote *The Gulag Archipelago*, a book about conditions in the Russian prison camps that stretched like a vast island chain through the frozen wastes of Siberia. This book, banned in Russia, became a best-seller in Western countries. Considering Solzhenitsyn too dangerous to remain inside Russia, the government deported him in 1973 upon his release from prison.

Socialist Filmmaking

Like other artists, film directors under the Communist regime were measured by their contribution and loyalty to the Communist government and to socialism. During the 1920s, filmmaker Sergei Eisenstein earned the state's approval with his films *Strike* and *Battleship Potemkin*, which detailed the struggles associated with the Bolshevik revolution.

In the 1930s, Eisenstein found the authorities strongly disapproving of his new work *Bezhin Meadow*, a film that the authorities did not see as fitting in the approved socialist realist style. Fearing for his career, and perhaps his life, Eisenstein responded in 1938 with *Alexander Nevsky*, a stirring account of Russians facing down Teutonic knights during the Middle Ages.

The censors and the moviegoing public saw the medieval Teutonic knights as representing the threat from Adolf Hitler, who had just ordered German troops to invade the Sudetenland in Central Europe. But in 1939, Stalin signed the Non-Aggression Pact with Nazi Germany. The Soviet and Nazi governments were now allies, and *Alexander Nevsky* disappeared from movie screens throughout Russia—only to return in 1941 when Hitler ordered the invasion of the Soviet Union.

Even private, everyday, mundane expression could be dangerous, especially under the reign of Joseph Stalin, who died in 1953. Andrei Sinyavsky recalls one such story:

> A man went to see his friend, an official of some kind, at his office but found that he was out. The official had promised to do something for his friend and then hadn't done it. The friend decided to leave him a note. For lack of anything better to write on, he grabbed a newspaper that was lying on the desk and scrawled: "You scum, you broke your promise!" He didn't notice Stalin's speech right next to his angry, impromptu note. But somebody else did—and called the NKVD. The poor devil was promptly arrested.[43]

Varieties of Censorship

The Communist government considered control of information essential to its hold on the country. Anyone found guilty of publishing or disseminating information deemed unofficial or seditious was liable to a prison term. Publications from non-Communist countries were banned, radio broadcasts of the Voice of America and the BBC were jammed, and foreign movies and television shows remained largely unknown to the average citizen. Those found with a copy of a banned book, or caught listening to a forbidden foreign radio broadcast, could be arrested.

Lenin himself had once published an underground newspaper known as *Iskra* ("The Spark"). But Lenin had also said, "Why should freedom of speech and freedom of the press be allowed? Why should a government which is doing what it believes is right allow itself to be criticized? It would not allow opposition by lethal weapons. Ideas are much more fatal things than guns."[44]

To set and enforce its restrictions on information, the Communist government set up Glavlit, a censorship bureau that issued an official index number for each approved book. This organization also published and distributed a book of prohibited topics for magazine and newspaper editors, television producers, book publishers –anyone connected with distributing information or entertainment to the public. The book laid down its restrictions for all forms of public speech, from television broadcasts to newspaper articles to stand-up comedy routines. Any government agency could request that a certain topic be banned, and such requests were usually approved.

As party ideology changed, writers found themselves and their works passing from official acceptance to disapproval. Many works praising Stalin, for example, were banned after 1956, when his successor Nikita Khrushchev began criticizing Stalin's character and policies.

Approved literature, even information already in the hands of private citizens, was always subject to official revision. One of the most famous revisions occurred after the death of KGB head Lavrenti Beria. All Russian citizens who had subscribed to the *Great Soviet Encyclopedia*, published by the official state publishing house, were mailed instructions to cut out and destroy four pages of volume 5 of the work (these pages contained an article praising Beria and his accomplishments). The encyclopedia owners were also told to replace the article with new text that skipped Beria entirely—a directive that officially banished from the encyclopedia and from the public record a man who had been one of the most powerful figures in the Soviet Union.

Samizdat Publishing

In the 1960s, Russian writers and readers coined a new term: *samizdat*, from the words *sam*, or "self," and *izdat*, or "publishing." Novels, stories, poems, and political tracts that could not be published officially were often published unofficially in samizdat form, often being reproduced on copying machines and then passed from one reader to another. Although photocopying equipment in Russia re-mained under lock and key at state and military offices, sympathetic civil servants and military personnel made copies voluntarily or for a fee. The copies themselves were nicknamed *kseroksi*, or "xeroxes." Some samizdat copies circulated to hundreds, even thousands, of readers, finding a much wider audience than official publications.

One of the perennial favorites of samizdat readers was *Animal Farm*, a novel by the British writer George Orwell that describes

Charlie Chaplin, Soviet Style

The Communist state judged all forms of art and entertainment by a political yardstick. Was a work sympathetic to socialism, especially through the use of socialist realism? Or was it merely a decadent, individualistic work with no social merit? The question was asked of paintings, musical compositions, books, and films. Even the "Little Tramp," Charlie Chaplin, could be interpreted according to Marxist-Leninist theory, at least according to the *Great Soviet Encyclopedia*:

"CHAPLIN, CHARLES SPENCER. Born April 16, 1889, in London; died Dec. 25, 1977, in Vevey, Switzerland. American film director, actor, and screenwriter.

A British national by birth, Chaplin was the son of music-hall entertainers. He made his stage debut at eight, and from 1907 to 1912 he worked his way up as a gifted comic actor. . . .

In Chaplin's films, the interweaving of the comic and the tragic perception of life grew increasingly evident, and the tendency toward social satire was clearly distinguishable. Chaplin's hero—Charlie the tramp—was an embodiment of the world's poor, the rejects of capitalist society.

Beginning in 1923, Chaplin produced the full-length films *A Woman of Paris* (1923), *The Gold Rush* (1925), and *The Circus* (1928), which are world masterpieces of screen comedy; their criticism of bourgeois society is combined with a profoundly humanist depiction of simple and unfortunate people."

According to the Soviets, Charlie Chaplin's character the "Little Tramp" epitomized the world's poor.

One of Russia's best-known writers, Alexander Solzhenitsyn, first arrived on the literary scene with a short novel, *One Day in the Life of Ivan Denisovich*. The book, which concerns a prisoner in a Siberian labor camp, found a wide audience within Russia, provoking the authorities to attempt to suppress it. Writer John Dornberg, in his book *The New Tsars*, quotes Solzhenitsyn on the Communist way of making an already-published book disappear from the public eye.

"The technique is to tell readers that the book is in the bindery, that it has been lent out, that there is momentarily no access to the shelves on which it is kept. Librarians are under instructions to refuse to circulate it. Here, for example, is a letter I received from a reader in the Crimea: 'I am an activist of our local library and was told confidentially of an order that your book be removed from circulation. One of the women working in the library wanted to present me with a souvenir copy of *Novy Mir* [a literary journal] containing *One Day in the Life of Ivan Denisovich*, because the library no longer needed it. Another librarian stopped her and told her that once a book had been assigned to the "special section" it was dangerous to make a present of it.'"

the everyday life of livestock on an imaginary totalitarian farm complete with corrupt bosses, informers, downtrodden masses, and working-class heroes. The works of Alexander Solzhenitsyn and certain Eastern European writers, such as the exiled Czech novelist Milan Kundera, passed all over Russia in dog-eared, heavily thumbed samizdat copies. In addition to fiction, the works of banned historians, mathematicians, and philosophers also survived in the samizdat world.

Samizdat publishing succeeded in spreading a wide variety of written works to curious readers throughout the country. It even created imitators in other artistic fields. During the 1970s, well after the origin of samizdat, came magnitizdat, from the word *magnitofon*, or tape recorder. Magnitizdat was the circulation of music on audio cassettes. In addition to many state-approved songs, Vladimir Vysotsky, one of the most famous musicians and stage actors in Russia, secretly recorded seditious ballads. These appeared on black-market cassettes and passed from one listener to the next.

Vysotsky: Protest Singer

For millions of Russians, Vysotsky was much more than a folksinger. His lyrics expressed a yearning for free expression and frustration with the Communist way of life. Author Kevin Klose explains Vysotsky's popularity as follows:

Appealing to millions of Soviets, Vysotsky had composed and sung dozens of tough-guy blue-collar songs describing their lives in the nation's factories, beer parlors, and dormitories. Many of his songs were available on officially approved record albums, which sold out instantly whenever they appeared on the shelves of the main Melodia record shop in central Moscow or elsewhere.[45]

The government music censors did not approve all of Vysotsky's works. His most popular works, and the ones best known to ordinary citizens, described life in labor and prison camps, where disobedient members of Russian society suffered long terms of re-education under harsh conditions.

Vysotsky songs that were not officially published circulated as magnitizdat recordings. In the 1970s, Vysotsky and singers Bulat Okudzhava and Alexander Galich rose to the top of the magnitizdat heap. By 1980, the year of Vysotsky's death, his music could be heard in homes, workplaces, university halls, nightclubs, and parks all over Communist Russia. The singer had become a very dangerous in-

Hundreds of thousands of adoring fans were present at the funeral for the singer Vladimir Vysotsky.

dividual in the eyes of Communist authorities. Despite their efforts at keeping the singer's Moscow funeral from becoming a public spectacle, word quickly spread, and hundreds of thousands of his fans came to pay their last respects.

Musical Life

Like writers and painters, Russian musicians belonged to a state-sponsored union. The state maintained several institutes of music, at which the nation's best performers and composers received their professional training. For the Russian musician, the highest achievement was a permanent position in a symphony orchestra, which provided a stable and secure living.

The real benefit of such a job, however, was the chance to travel abroad. Members of the orchestra that accompanied the famed Bolshoi Ballet considered themselves lucky to tour in Western Europe and the United States. (The state exported the Bolshoi Ballet, like the Moscow Circus, to foreign audiences in an effort to persuade foreigners of the vitality and freedom of the arts under the Communist system.) While traveling, the musicians were given a certain amount of foreign currency to spend as they wished. As much as possible, the money was hoarded and brought home, where valued goods could only be bought in stores that only accepted foreign currency. David K. Shipler, in his book *Russia: Broken Idols, Solemn Dreams*, explained the system:

> If you were doing a tour in the United States, for example, you received a stipend of $19 a day, $25 on concert days. The cash was supposed to go for lunch and dinner—you didn't have to pay for

Members of the famed Bolshoi Ballet prepare for a performance.

travel, hotels, and breakfast—so many musicians tried to survive with as little restaurant eating as possible, practically starving themselves by eating cans of fish and hunks of salami and cheese carried with them from the Soviet Union, saving as many of the dollars as they could to buy clothing, tape recorders, and stereo sets for themselves, friends, and acquaintances who did them favors back home.[46]

The trip to the West was one of the great benefits of being a professional musician in Communist Russia. At the same time, per-formers knew that, at any moment, their privilege of foreign travel could be taken away by the authorities, for almost any reason. A show of disloyalty, a word of criticism, an improper attitude—all could bring the punishment of having the right to travel taken away. There were a thousand such ways of keeping Russian citizens obedient, and instances of punishment were made as public as possible by the party and its Communist officials. The threat of losing one's privileges proved to be one of the most effective ways of enforcing loyalty to the state and to the Communist system.

Enforcing the Soviet State

The people of Russia had always been accustomed to heavy-handed law enforcement and to the sight of uniformed authorities. In tsarist times, police officers, both uniformed and undercover, kept tabs on all those considered subversive or disloyal to the regime. In Communist Russia, police officers directed traffic, guarded museums and important buildings, accompanied officials in their automobiles, and patrolled the important streets and squares of every city. Their orders were to keep order, restrain troublemakers, supervise public gatherings of any and all kinds, and prevent or thwart crime. For the most part, they were well paid, well equipped, and efficient, and the Communist government often boasted of a serious-crime rate far lower than that of Western capitalist countries.

Russia's leaders often held up the low crime rate as proof that the Communist system was superior to that of the West. Communist leaders also proudly pointed to the loyalty and civic-mindedness of party members. There was a gimmick to this claim, however, as explained by the "dissident" writer Alexander Ushakov, who was accused of being a dangerous and subversive individual:

> You are expelled from the party first . . . and only then turned over to the investigators. Only nonmembers are tried. As a result—statistically—the crime rate among members of the CPSU [Communist Party

Russian police students attend traffic control class.

of the Soviet Union] is zero. The formula "A criminal can't be a communist" is simply reversed: "A communist can't be a criminal." He can't even have his own opinion of the organization to which he belongs. A personal opinion of the CPSU is also a crime, and that is what I was charged with.[47]

Unlike Communist Party members, ordinary citizens were subject to immediate arrest for illegal activities. Yet because the laws of Communist Russia forebade people from owning certain personal property, buying and selling goods in a certain way, and living or traveling in the wrong place, there was a tremendous amount of wrongdoing at every level of society. One Russian citizen put it this way:

> Everyone is a criminal. To do more than merely survive a person requires use of the black market and access to foreign currency. He must gain and use influence and bribe in small but illegal ways. To drive a car, to go to the opera on a good night, to get edible food, to place one's son in a good school—all that makes you commit crimes. . . . Once you do one thing, take one privilege, you're lost. Someone always knows you've gone out of bounds. You can be brought up on charges any time.[48]

The Secret Police

One arm of law enforcement was not easily seen but very well known to every citizen. The "secret" police went about their business in plain clothes, and their duty was to protect the Communist state itself from all known or suspected opponents. The underground police

Glasnost and the Meltdown

The explosion and meltdown at the Chernobyl nuclear plant in 1986 had lasting effects on politics and on freedom in Communist Russia. For several days after the disaster, the Russian news media gave no information whatsoever about the burning plant, about the radiation leaking into the air, or about the great danger faced by millions of Russian and Soviet citizens. Just a few days after the event, a May Day parade in Kiev, just ninety miles away, went ahead on the orders of the local Communist party boss, while Party officials evacuated their own families from the city.

The West didn't know about Chernobyl until fallout reached Sweden, two days after the accident. Even then, the Soviet media released only a vague acknowledgment that some kind of mishap had occurred. The entire nuclear industry of the Soviet Union was top secret. Even the engineers and foremen working at Chernobyl were not aware of certain risks they had encountered while running the test that caused the explosion.

Mikhail Gorbachev, the new first secretary of the Communist Party, saw the Chernobyl disaster as a condemnation of the old, secret way of withholding news and information from the public. As a consequence, he gave orders for a new era of glasnost, or "openness." He replaced former loyal editors with new, more independent editors at leading Soviet journals. The government censors granted these editors greater freedom to run articles criticizing the failings of the Communist system. Glasnost brought more open journalism and writing to Russia. As a result, a better-informed public grew even more critical of their society and their system of government.

were ever watchful for signs of opposition to the state and its practices. Suspects included workers who complained or whose production did not meet quotas; artists whose paintings or movies did not meet with official approval; ordinary citizens who traveled abroad and brought home banned goods; party members who formed friendships with suspected anti-Communists; and any individual who expressed anger or disappointment—in public or private—with the state. Anyone who met informally with foreigners within Russia also ran the risk of coming under watchful eyes.

The secret police kept files on all those identified as suspects. They used spies—neighbors, coworkers, friends—to keep tabs on suspects, assigning agents to follow the more important persons around town. The police carried out many routine searches of homes and apartments, looking for subversive material such as Western books, Bibles and religious tracts, letters received from other suspects within Russia, or other signs of antigovernment activity. They also used listening devices to eavesdrop on telephone calls and conversations held within hotel rooms and apartments.

The secret police used intimidation and the threat of arrest to keep citizens in line. Russians always carefully measured the possible legal consequences of their actions: traveling, reading, speaking in public, or trading their goods or services informally. Being taken into custody meant, at the least, spending a few hours with an experienced police interrogator, who was free to ask any sort of question about one's private or public life. The suspect was obliged to answer but did not have the right to know the charges against him or her or to have a lawyer present. The police, on the other hand, were free to use all manner of coercion, from a long confinement in a small or darkened room to physical torture. In many cases, police interrogation was a mere formality, carried out to obtain the suspect's signature on a confession, which would then be used to prove the crime with which he or she had already been charged.

Under Suspicion

Even suspects freed by the police knew they would remain under suspicion and that they always risked another arrest and interrogation session. The harassment could continue for months, even years. The suspect might be forced to attend "re-education" classes, at which participants made confessions of their wrongdoing and instructors used heavy-handed methods to instill "correct" thinking.

After re-education, a suspect remained a suspect. Privileges granted by the state, such as the right to drive or the right to travel, might be taken away suddenly, with no reason given. Work became more difficult, as coworkers remained aloof, for fear that they would become entangled with the police. Once an individual came under suspicion, it was almost impossible to regain a normal place in society.

In other cases, arrest meant imprisonment and exile. Continuing a tradition of the old Russian Empire, the Communist government sent its political prisoners as far as possible to the gulags of cold and distant Siberia. There, prisoners labored in unhealthy and dangerous conditions to build public projects such as dams or railroads. Many worked in terrifying underground mines or were forced to crush rock or fell trees. They were given only enough food to survive and only enough clothing to keep from freezing to death. Prisoners could write no letters, make no telephone calls, and make no other sort of contact with their friends and families. In effect, the

The modern era of Russian dissidence began with Nikita Khrushchev's "Secret Speech" delivered to a closed session of Communist Party leaders in February 1956. In the speech, Khrushchev shocked his listeners by directly criticizing Joseph Stalin and the harsh repression of Stalin's regime during the 1930s. Over time the text of the Secret Speech spread to low-level politicians, factory managers, and gradually ordinary readers, who discovered that the Communist Party did make mistakes and pursue wrong policies, as admitted for the first time by its own leader.

After the Secret Speech, Russians began to sense a gradual easing in the state's strict censorship. Writers in official party newspapers began to cautiously criticize the state's policies, and dissidents began circulating their writings through the samizdat underground. Although he had sought only to strengthen the Communist Party, Nikita Khrushchev initiated an era of dissidence that eventually flowered into open rebellion in the 1980s.

Nikita Khrushchev

political prisoner became a dead person, an individual who had completely disappeared from home and society.

The Dissident Life

Dissidents in Communist Russia were subject to harassment and spying by the officers of the KGB, the state secret police force. Like any person suspected of a political crime, they could be arrested without warning, put through a trial at which no defense was allowed and the verdict was predetermined, and banished to a labor camp. The state sentenced some dissidents to psychiatric hospitals to serve out long sentences as patients. They were kept quiet through medication and remained under the close supervision of doctors and nurses. Those who did not lose their minds after years of confinement and heavy medication found themselves shunned—as both politically dangerous and insane—upon returning to society.

On occasion, the homes and apartments of dissidents were searched for evidence of their subversive activities. Waiting for a knock at the door was a daily facet of life for those singled out by the KGB for surveillance as dissidents. Even if it didn't end in an arrest, a search could bring the loss of letters, books, documents, and other personal possessions. Elena Bonner, the wife of the dissident physicist Andrei Sakharov, recalled one such search in her book *Alone Together*:

> I was awakened by a ring at the door in the morning. When I opened it, Kolesnikov [a KGB officer] came in with two women, one in a police uniform, several men, and two women from our building as witnesses. They presented me with a search warrant. This was around nine o'clock, and the search began, a long, boring one. I think they themselves were tired of digging around in Andrei's papers. They took away an enormous amount, listed as 319 items, several of the items were files of up to three hundred pages. They removed many books, all the English and German ones. They also took the typewriter, the tape recorder, the camera and movie camera, and, most important, the radio.[49]

Dissidents, known for their words and writings and marked out by the security police, were not the only ones to fear a sudden appearance by the police. A Moscow journalist named Alexander Milchakov, whose father was arrested in his home and sent to a prison camp for fifteen years, described the fears of ordinary Russians:

> People didn't sleep, because every night there were arrests. These arrests had one unique feature: the sound of boots booming up the staircase. When the NKVD men climbed the stairs, the tenants racked their brains trying to figure out

Andrei Sakharov and Elena Bonner were subjected to frequent searches by security police.

where they were headed. Would they stop one flight higher? or lower? They didn't take the elevator—there was some kind of order against this, probably for fear of breakdowns.[50]

Early Signs of the Downfall of Russian Communism

When Mikhail Gorbachev came to power as the leader of the Soviet Union in 1985, control of information began to lessen. Little by little, the government relaxed its strict censorship of the press and of broadcast media. In the newspapers, writers began to criticize state policies and to reveal bribery and official corruption. To become a dissident in Russia gradually became fashionable, rather than dangerous. Many Russians prepared themselves for the end of the Communist system. Loyal party members gradually turned against the system, expressing their long-standing doubts about Communist economics or about the wisdom and incorruptibility of the nation's leaders. Not in all cases were such dissidents sincere, as pointed out by Yelena Khanga in *Soul to Soul*:

> It's been truly amazing to find out how many of my contemporaries were dissidents all along. They were only pretending to enjoy the dachas and other privileges—the vacations abroad or in the Crimea, designer clothes—acquired by their parents through a lifetime of service to the state! They were really members of a secret underground dedicated to overthrowing a rotten system! Why, the KGB was about to arrest them on the very day Gorbachev came to power! It's amazing the system didn't crumble long ago, since the country was populated by

so many brave people. Why didn't I know any of them then?[51]

The Glasnost Era

By the end of the 1980s, dissidents made up a majority of the Russian population. Throughout the country, ordinary people compared their lives with those of ordinary people living in non-Communist societies, and they grew angry. The utopia predicted by Marx and Lenin still seemed a long way off; in the meantime, food and goods remained scarce, and workers earned meager salaries and struggled to support their families.

At the same time, Gorbachev and other Russian leaders were trying to change the Communist system in order to save it. They adopted two keywords for their actions: *glasnost*, signifying openness, and *perestroika*, signifying economic reform.

Under glasnost, Russians did enjoy access to television, movies, books, and magazines from Western Europe and the United States. For the first time, rock and jazz musicians toured the country. New American movies replaced the old black-and-white films from the 1930s and 1940s in Russian cinemas. In Moscow, a McDonalds restaurant opened. This new imported culture opened a window to a completely different way of life, one that had seemed very distant to Russian citizens just a few years before.

The End Comes Suddenly

The reforms and the lifting of censorship did not bring the hoped-for result of better economic conditions and the survival of communism. Instead, shortages of food and consumer

During the glasnost era Russians began to enjoy more access to television, books, and Western influences such as McDonalds restaurant food.

goods continued, factories and farms produced less, and ordinary people grew even more frustrated. Buying imported goods re-

mained almost impossible for the ordinary Russian worker, whose salary remained fixed and low. Because Russia had refused to trade with the West for so long, the Russian currency, the ruble, held little value. To buy certain things, even in their own country, many Russians had to use German marks or U.S. dollars, which they acquired on trips abroad or on the underground currency market. Or they had to barter their goods and services and not use currency at all. Russians felt humiliated at this loss of sovereignty in the face of wealthier Western countries, and many ordinary citizens began to feel that the Communist system should not be preserved at all.

When the Communist regimes of Eastern Europe began to fall in the late 1980s, Russians grew more hopeful for a change of government in their own country. Finally, in the summer of 1991, the tensions building inside the country erupted. A group of Russian politicians and military leaders opposed to Gorbachev's reforms tried, and failed, to take over the government. One by one, the republics making up the Soviet Union declared their independence. Finally, on December 25, the Communist flag flying over the Kremlin was lowered, and the Communist experiment in Russia and throughout the Soviet Union came to an end.

Notes

Introduction: The People and the State

1. Quoted in Jeane Kirkpatrick, *The Withering Away of the Totalitarian State—and Other Surprises*. Washington, DC: AEI Press, 1990, p. 1.
2. Quoted in Robert Payne, *The Life and Death of Lenin*. New York: Simon and Schuster, 1964, p. 419.

Chapter 1: Life in the City

3. Michael Dobbs, *Down with Big Brother: The Fall of the Soviet Empire*. New York: Alfred A. Knopf, 1997, p. 91.
4. Quoted in Richard Lourie, *Russia Speaks: An Oral History from the Revolution to the Present*. New York: HarperCollins, 1991, p. 15.
5. Andrei Sinyavsky, *Soviet Civilization: A Cultural History*. New York: Arcade Publishing, 1990, p. 169.
6. Sinyavsky, *Soviet Civilization*, p. 165.
7. Harrison Salisbury, *American in Russia*. New York: Harper & Brothers, pp. 223–24.
8. Jo Durden-Smith, *Russia: A Long-Shot Romance*. New York: Alfred A. Knopf, 1994, p. 18.
9. J. N. Westwood, *Russia, 1917–1964*. New York: Harper & Row, 1966, p. 49.
10. Scott Shane, *Dismantling Utopia: How Information Ended the Soviet Union*. Chicago: Ivan R. Dee, 1994, p. 3.
11. Quoted in David K. Shipler, *Russia: Broken Idols, Solemn Dreams*. New York: New York Times Book Co., 1983, p. 89.
12. Westwood, *Russia, 1917–1964*, p. 70.

Chapter 2: Life in the Country

13. Salisbury, *American in Russia*, p. 111.
14. Dobbs, *Down with Big Brother*, p. 4.
15. Serge Schmemann, *Echoes of a Native Land: Two Centuries of a Russian Village*. New York: Alfred A. Knopf, 1997, p. 212.
16. David Remnick, *Lenin's Tomb: The Last Days of the Soviet Empire*. New York: Random House, 1993, p. 210.
17. Alan Bookbinder, Olivia Lichtenstein, and Richard Denton, *Comrades: Portraits of Soviet Life*. New York: New American Library, 1985, p. 128.
18. Dobbs, *Down with Big Brother*, p. 27.
19. Georges Bortoli, *Moscow and Leningrad Observed*. New York: Oxford University Press, 1975, p. 36.
20. John Dornberg, *The New Tsars: Russia Under Stalin's Heirs*. Garden City, NY: Doubleday, 1972, pp. 398–99.

Chapter 3: Education

21. Sinyavsky, *Soviet Civilization*, p. 41.
22. Remnick, *Lenin's Tomb*, pp. 37–38.
23. Yelena Khanga, with Susan Jacoby, *Soul to Soul: The Story of a Black Russian American Family, 1865–1992*. New York: W. W. Norton, 1992, p. 127.
24. Adam Hochschild, *The Unquiet Ghost: Russians Remember Stalin*. New York: Viking Penguin, 1994, pp. 132–33.
25. Quoted in Bookbinder et al., *Comrades*, p. 14.
26. Quoted in Joan Hasler, *The Making of Russia: From Prehistory to Modern Times*. New York: Delacorte Press, 1969, p. 189.
27. Shipler, *Russia*, p. 351.

28. Hasler, *The Making of Russia*, pp. 192–93.

Chapter 4: Work in Communist Russia

29. Nikita Khrushchev, *Khrushchev Remembers*. Boston: Little, Brown, 1970, p. 17.
30. Yuri Tarnopolsky, *Memoirs of 1984*. Lanham, MD: University Press of America, Inc., 1993, p. 144.
31. Quoted in Michael Binyon, *Life in Russia*. New York: Pantheon Books, 1983, p. 258.

Chapter 5: Sports and Leisure Time

32. Salisbury, *American in Russia*, pp. 261–62.
33. Bortoli, *Moscow and Leningrad Observed*, p. 36.
34. Hasler, *The Making of Russia*, pp. 196–97.
35. Bortoli, *Moscow and Leningrad Observed*, p. 31.
36. Shipler, *Russia*, p. 251.

Chapter 6: Religion

37. Dornberg, *The New Tsars*, p. 26.
38. Chaim Potok, *The Gates of November: Chronicles of the Slepak Family*. New York: Alfred A. Knopf, 1996, p. 65.
39. Bortoli, *Moscow and Leningrad Observed*, p. 11.
40. David Satter, *Age of Delirium: The Decline and Fall of the Soviet Union*, New York: Alfred A. Knopf, 1996, p. 95.

41. Andrew Wachtel and Eugene Zykov, *At the Dawn of Glasnost: Soviet Portraits*. San Francisco: Proctor Jones, 1988, p. 67.

Chapter 7: Art, Literature, and Music

42. Westwood, *Russia, 1917–1964*, p. 108.
43. Sinyavsky, *Soviet Civilization*, p. 89.
44. Quoted in Shane, *Dismantling Utopia*, p. 50.
45. Kevin Klose, *Russia and the Russians: Inside the Closed Society*. New York: W. W. Norton, 1984, p. 284.
46. Shipler, *Russia*, p. 356.

Chapter 8: Enforcing the Soviet State

47. Alexander A. Ushakov, *In the Gunsight of the KGB: The Story of One Man's Spectacular Escape Across the Most Heavily Guarded Border in the World*. New York: Alfred A. Knopf, 1989, p. 144.
48. Jay Martin, *Winter Dreams: An American in Moscow*. Boston: Houghton Mifflin, 1979, p. 83.
49. Elena Bonner, *Alone Together*. New York: Alfred A. Knopf, 1986, pp. 71–72.
50. Quoted in Hochschild, *The Unquiet Ghost*, p. 97.
51. Khanga, *Soul to Soul*, p. 176.

For Further Reading

Alan Bookbinder, Olivia Lichtenstein, and Richard Denton, *Comrades: Portraits of Soviet Life*. New York: New American Library, 1985. A series of first-person accounts of Russians of all ages and from all walks of life, emphasizing progress and achievements made under the Soviet regime.

Geography Department, Lerner Publications. *Russia*. Minneapolis: Lerner Publications, 1992. A concise treatment of the Russian land, people, history, and economy, prepared immediately after the fall of communism.

Leo Gruliow and the Editors of Time-Life Books, *Moscow*. Amsterdam: Time-Life Books, 1977. A lively, well-written, touristic account of the Russian capital and its unique institutions, illustrated with excellent photographs.

Yelena Khanga, with Susan Jacoby, *Soul to Soul: The Story of a Black Russian American Family, 1865–1992*. New York: W. W. Norton, 1992. The story of an African American family that migrates to Russia during the 1920s, and whose descendants experience a mixture of suspicion and curiosity on the part of their native Russian friends, acquaintances, and officials.

Richard Lourie, *Russia Speaks: An Oral History from the Revolution to the Present*. New York: HarperCollins, 1991. Russians speak candidly about their lives and their problems, their hard work, their families, and their attitudes toward socialism and the Communist regime they live under.

Kathleen Berton Murrell, *Russia: Eyewitness Books*. New York: Alfred A. Knopf, 1998. A busy photographic survey of Russian history and culture as seen through hundreds of artifacts, artworks, photographs, posters, and so on, each given an informative caption.

Abraham Resnick, *The Union of Soviet Socialist Republics: A Survey from 1917 to 1991*. Chicago: Childrens Press, 1992. A reference-style book on Russian geography, society, culture, economics, and everyday life, with a final chapter on the end of communism.

John Roberson, *Transforming Russia, 1682 to 1991*. New York: Atheneum, 1992. An excellent and readable description of Russian history from Peter the Great to Mikhail Gorbachev.

Serge Schmemann, *Echoes of a Native Land: Two Centuries of a Russian Village*. New York: Alfred A. Knopf, 1997. The author details his family history and the story of the village of Sergiyeskoye, from tsarist times through the revolution and the displacements caused by collectivization.

Works Consulted

Michael Binyon, *Life in Russia*. New York: Pantheon Books, 1983. The Moscow correspondent of the *London Times* describes in detail daily life and Russian attitudes toward the work, the state, the arts, religion, the role of women, and the nations of the West.

Elena Bonner, *Alone Together*. New York: Alfred A. Knopf, 1986. The dramatic first-person account of Elena Bonner, wife of dissident Russian scientist Andrei Sakharov, and the couple's tribulations at the hands of the Soviet government and the KGB.

Georges Bortoli, *Moscow and Leningrad Observed*. New York: Oxford University Press, 1975. A photo essay on the two principal Russian cities, contrasting their monumental and imperial past with their socialist present.

Michael Dobbs, *Down with Big Brother: The Fall of the Soviet Empire*. New York: Alfred A. Knopf, 1997. A detailed journalistic account of the last years of the Communist empire in Russia and Central Europe.

John Dornberg, *The New Tsars: Russia Under Stalin's Heirs*. Garden City, NY: Doubleday, 1972. A political essay on the works and ideas of Soviet leaders after Joseph Stalin.

John Dunlop, *The Rise of Russia and the Fall of the Soviet Empire*. Princeton, NJ: Princeton University Press, 1993. A book on the emergence of Russian culture and nationalism in the aftermath of the collapse of the Soviet Union.

Jo Durden-Smith, *Russia: A Long-Shot Romance*. New York: Alfred A. Knopf, 1994. Assigned to write an article on the city of Leningrad in 1988, the author becomes immersed in Russian culture, falls in love, and eventually joins the society he had only intended to observe.

The Great Soviet Encyclopedia. Third Edition, vol. 29. New York: Macmillan, 1982. A 30-volume collection of more than one hundred thousand entries on economics, science, and culture, published at the direction of the Central Committee of the Communist Party of the Soviet Union. An exhaustive compendium of knowledge and analysis based on the advantages of the socialist system, the problems and future prospects of the international revolutionary movement, and the deepening crisis of world capitalism.

Joan Hasler, *The Making of Russia: From Prehistory to Modern Times*. New York: Delacorte Press, 1969. An overview of Russian history and a brief description of Russian life and society under Communist rule.

Adam Hochschild, *The Unquiet Ghost: Russians Remember Stalin*. New York: Viking Penguin, 1994. A tour among Russians who remember, with both nostalgia and terror, the years they spent living under the reign of Joseph Stalin, the Soviet dictator responsible for the execution, starvation, and imprisonment of millions of Russian citizens in the 1930s.

Ryszard Kapuscinski, *Imperium*. New York: Alfred A. Knopf, 1994. A memoir of the author's childhood in the city of Pinsk, and his travels through Russia and the Soviet Empire in the 1960s and early 1990s.

Nikita Khrushchev, *Khrushchev Remembers*. Boston: Little, Brown, 1970. The memoirs of the Soviet premier who, at the twentieth Party Congress in 1956, openly criticized the reign of Joseph Stalin in the 1930s and 1940s, an action that paved the way for partial reforms in Russia's Communist society.

Jeane Kirkpatrick, *The Withering Away of the Totalitarian State—and Other Surprises*. Washington, DC: AEI Press, 1990. A former U.S. representative to the United Nations describes the inherent contradictions and fallacies of Marxist ideology that brought about the collapse of the Soviet regime.

Kevin Klose, *Russia and the Russians: Inside the Closed Society*. New York: W. W. Norton, 1984. The Moscow bureau chief of the *Washington Post* describes Communist society as he experienced it during his years as a reporter from 1977 to 1981.

Jay Martin, *Winter Dreams: An American in Moscow*. Boston: Houghton Mifflin, 1979. A professor of American literature journeys to Moscow, where he becomes intimately and sometimes dangerously involved with the lives of Russian citizens.

Robert Payne, *The Life and Death of Lenin*. New York: Simon and Schuster, 1964. A long and meticulously researched account of the founding father of the Soviet Union and Communist Russia.

Chaim Potok, *The Gates of November: Chronicles of the Slepak Family*. New York: Alfred A. Knopf, 1996. An American novelist compiles a nonfiction work recording the adventures of the Slepak family, Russian Jews who suffer persecution as "refuseniks" and who are marked out as criminals for their desire to emigrate to Israel.

David Remnick, *Lenin's Tomb: The Last Days of the Soviet Empire*. New York: Random House, 1993. A vivid description of the crumbling of the Soviet regime during the late 1980s, when ordinary Russians openly questioned the state's official version of their own history as well as socialist dogma.

Harrison Salisbury, *American in Russia*. New York: Harper & Brothers, 1954. A journalist and Moscow bureau chief for the *New York Times* describes personal experiences of Communist government and society after spending five years of his life in the Soviet Union.

David Satter, *Age of Delirium: The Decline and Fall of the Soviet Union*. New York: Alfred A. Knopf, 1996. A journalist gives an account of the deception and delusion of ordinary life and work in Communist Russia during the 1980s.

Leona and Jerrold Schechter, *An American Family in Moscow*. Boston: Little, Brown, 1975. The account of the everyday life and experiences of an American family immersed full-time in Russian society.

Scott Shane, *Dismantling Utopia: How Information Ended the Soviet Union*. Chicago: Ivan R. Dee, 1994. A description of the era of 1980s perestroika and glasnost, emphasizing the revolutionary role of print and broadcast media and how it brought about the end of Russia's Communist government.

David K. Shipler, *Russia: Broken Idols, Solemn Dreams*. New York: New York Times Book Co., 1983. A chronicle of everyday life in Communist Russia at the important turning point in the early 1980s, when Russian society opened up to the West and when partial and ineffective reforms, economic stagnation, and popular discontent began undermining the Communist regime.

Andrei Sinyavsky, *Soviet Civilization: A Cultural History*. New York: Arcade Publishing, 1990. One of Russia's leading dissident writers gives an intelligent and penetrating look at life and art under the Communist system.

Hedrick Smith, *The New Russians*. New York: Random House, 1990. Using interviews he took in Russia in the late 1980s, the author describes the debates, conflicts, and jealousies among Russian business and political leaders, as well as nationalist movements that gradually tore apart the Soviet Union.

Yuri Tarnopolsky, *Memoirs of 1984*. Lanham, MD: University Press of America, 1993. A refusenik details his arrest and trial as well as harrowing experiences as a zek, or prisoner, within the vast network of Siberian prison camps.

Alexander A. Ushakov, *In the Gunsight of the KGB: The Story of One Man's Spectacular Escape Across the Most Heavily Guarded Border in the World*. New York: Alfred A. Knopf, 1989. A first-person account of the arrest and trial of a professor at the Odessa Naval Academy who, instead of accepting a long prison term, made his way across a mountainous and heavily guarded border to freedom.

Leonid Vladimirov, *The Russians*. New York: Frederick A. Praeger, 1968. An in-depth portrait of Russian society by a factory foreman, Stalinist-era prisoner, and leading newspaper editor who defected in 1966. His firsthand experience of Russian society at almost all levels and settings gives Vladimirov's book credibility and great authority.

Andrew Wachtel and Eugene Zykov, *At the Dawn of Glasnost: Soviet Portraits*. San Francisco: Proctor Jones, 1988. A photo essay that describes the working lives of people from all walks of life in Communist Russia and several other republics of the Soviet Union.

J. N. Westwood, *Russia, 1917–1964*. New York: Harper & Row, 1966. An outdated but useful and informative summary of Soviet history and Russian society from the revolution through the Khrushchev years.

Index

Picture Credits

About the Author

Thomas Streissguth is a critically acclaimed author of nonfiction books in the fields of history, geography, biography, and current events. He has written juvenile books for all grade levels and has also produced reference and nonfiction work for adults. He has traveled widely in Europe and the Middle East and has worked as a teacher, journalist, and editor. In 1999, he founded a summer language school in northern France, where he regularly travels with his family.